Thilo Klein

WHY DO INDIA'S URBAN POOR CHOOSE TO GO PRIVATE?

Health Policy Simulations in Slums of Hyderabad

ibidem-Verlag
Stuttgart

Bibliografische Information der Deutschen Nationalbibliothek
Die Deutsche Nationalbibliothek verzeichnet diese Publikation in der
Deutschen Nationalbibliografie; detaillierte bibliografische Daten sind im
Internet über http://dnb.d-nb.de abrufbar.

Bibliographic information published by the Deutsche Nationalbibliothek
Die Deutsche Nationalbibliothek lists this publication in the Deutsche Nationalbibliografie;
detailed bibliographic data are available in the Internet at http://dnb.d-nb.de.

∞

Gedruckt auf alterungsbeständigem, säurefreien Papier
Printed on acid-free paper

ISSN: 2190-2291

ISBN-13: 978-3-8382-0238-9

© *ibidem*-Verlag
Stuttgart 2012

Alle Rechte vorbehalten

Das Werk einschließlich aller seiner Teile ist urheberrechtlich geschützt. Jede Verwertung außerhalb der engen Grenzen des Urheberrechtsgesetzes ist ohne Zustimmung des Verlages unzulässig und strafbar. Dies gilt insbesondere für Vervielfältigungen, Übersetzungen, Mikroverfilmungen und elektronische Speicherformen sowie die Einspeicherung und Verarbeitung in elektronischen Systemen.

All rights reserved. No part of this publication may be reproduced, stored in or introduced into a retrieval system, or transmitted, in any form, or by any means (electronical, mechanical, photocopying, recording or otherwise) without the prior written permission of the publisher. Any person who does any unauthorized act in relation to this publication may be liable to criminal prosecution and civil claims for damages.

Printed in Germany

Contents

1 Introduction   1

2 Literature   3

3 Theory   7
    3.1 Stated preference theory 7
    3.2 Extensions to Neoclassical consumer theory 9
       3.2.1 Lancaster's approach 9
       3.2.2 Discrete choice 10
       3.2.3 Random utility maximization 12
    3.3 Divisible attributes 13
    3.4 Choice under uncertainty 18

4 Empirical Analysis   21
    4.1 Data 21
    4.2 Survey design 22
    4.3 Econometric model 24
       4.3.1 Binary choice model 24
       4.3.2 Bayesian hierarchical logit 25
    4.4 Validity issues 26
       4.4.1 Lexicographic preferences 26
       4.4.2 Further validity issues 29
    4.5 Results 31
       4.5.1 Market segmentation 31
       4.5.2 Insurance demand of the poor 34
       4.5.3 Market simulations 38

5   Conclusion   45
    References   46
    Annex A: Reference Card   53
    Annex B: Regression Results   55
    Annex C: R Script   57
    Annex D: Survey Questionnaires   61

List of Tables

4.1	Tests for lexicographic preferences	27
4.2	Two-way table of relative frequencies by income and literacy status	29
4.3	Correlation matrix of individual-level part-worths	33
4.4	Part-worths	35
4.5	Hospital options for simulation and simulated market share	39
5.1	Willingness to pay (in Rs) by demographics for discrete attribute levels	55

List of Figures

3.1 Goods and characteristics space in Lancaster's model of consumer behaviour 8
3.2 Effect of ex-post adjustment 14
3.3 Risk averse utility function 18

4.1 Sample choice cards 22
4.2 Utility functions by income 37
4.3 Policy simulation for option "Govt Hospital" 41

5.1 Reference card 53

Acknowledgements

I am greatly indebted to my academic supervisor, Dr Paul Kattuman. The discussions with him form the foundations of this dissertation and I would like to express my gratitude for giving me his time and intellectual support. Special thanks also go to my course director, Prof Stefan Scholtes, and participants of the Management Science and Operations Seminar for extremely valuable comments during my research progress presentations.

This dissertation would not have been possible without the support of three very generous sponsors.

First, I owe gratitude to the Quintiles Fund for Health Management and the Center for Health Leadership at Judge Business School for partially funding my MPhil studies at Cambridge University.

Second, the scholarship awarded by PlaNet Finance's University Meets Microfinance Project supported my field research in India in both material and non-material aspects.

Finally, I am grateful to microlender Spandana in Hyderabad for generous technical support. Its people made this study possible. I am especially indebted to Syed Shoebullah, Lansing Lee, Prakash Satyavageeswaran, and the five interviewers who spent their days out in the field during two months of heavy monsoon rains.

Editorial

Thilo Klein's dissertation is focussed on a fundamentally important empirical puzzle in the context of "consumer behaviour" with respect to health services at the "bottom of the pyramid". It is well known that in many developing countries, even the abjectly poor show marked preferences for privately provided health services compared to public offerings. This is so even though the private health sector is more expensive and generally employs less-qualified professionals who are demonstrably more responsive to patients' perceived medical needs. This dissertation reports on an empirical project that seeks to explain why this is the case. The specific context is maternity health services in the urban slums of Hyderabad in India.

The dissertation addresses the broad issue of choices available to poor consumers between various health care packages through a clearly posed empirical question. What are consumers' levels of "willingness-to-pay" for different quality levels of the various attributes that combine to form maternity care packages? For example, attributes such as privacy, professionalism of team, continuity of medical attention, guaranteed availability of medicines and medical equipment, and the price of the health care package. Answers to this question can be developed to yield comparative statics of market shares for a wide variety of hypothetical maternity care packages that are differentiated in terms of the way attribute qualities are combined.

To obtain valid answers to the above empirical question, it is necessary to obtain rich data on the willingness of consumers to substitute between quality levels of different attributes that are in health care packages. Discrete Choice Experiments are used to elicit "stated preferences" from a large sample of respondents. The survey instrument developed for this purpose was carefully adapted to the low literacy context of urban slums, and refined using pilot surveys and expert opinions. The resulting rich data set is used to estimate a characteristics-based random utility consumer-demand model. The consumer theoretic motivation for the econometric model is novel in distinguishing between divisible (for example, medicines) and indivisible (for example, privacy) characteristics bundled together in health care packages. From the vantage point of the model, it is easy to appreciate that consumer choice between health care packages depends crucially on the fact that divisible attributes such as "medicines and equipment" may also be subject to uncertain "demand". If such an attribute is not comprehensively provided for in a chosen package, then this component will need to be purchased ex post.

This is the crux of a highly plausible explanation to the puzzle of poor consumers' predilection for private health care. A higher degree of (empirically inferred) risk-aversion of the poorer consumers is sufficient to lead them to choose health care packages that "insure" medicines and medical equipment, albeit at a higher package price, over cheaper health care packages that leave them bearing the risk of having to purchase supplementary medication to some uncertain extent. It is a significant and novel finding that even the poorest of the poor are willing to pay for such "insurance". Indeed they are willing to pay more than they actually spend for extra medication. This suggests a strong policy conclusion: the current focus on providing free basic medication to the poor is misplaced. A much more welfare-effective policy could be built around fairly priced insurance cover for medicines and equipment.

This dissertation contributes very significant original insights to private provision of health services at the bottom of the pyramid. The model and methods can be applied to other areas where there is private provision of public services – such as education.

Dr Paul Kattuman
Cambridge, 15 July 2010

Abstract

This dissertation contributes to the resolution of a puzzle. Why does a large proportion of India's urban poor choose to pay for private health services when public services are essentially free of charge? Drawing from previous research, this study takes the underprovision of the medication component in public health packages as a starting point. Field evidence shows that patients in public health facilities often have to get external medication, whereas private hospitals offer a menu of pre-specified care packages.

We contribute an answer as to why the poor choose to go private by investigating their risk-aversion and demand for insurance in the choice of health facilities.

In discrete choice experiments on maternity care in the slums of Hyderabad, we find that the lowest income group attaches significantly higher importance to "full medication" maternity care packages. In line with Expected Utility theory, we further find empirical evidence that this insurance demand of the poor is partially explained by their risk-aversion.

Using health care market simulations, we show that sufficient provision of medicines can increase the market share of a public hospital option from the current 57% up to 100%. Further, "willingness to pay" estimates for such a medical insurance package exceed the median price currently paid for external medication by a large margin.

These findings suggest that an effective pro-poor policy should provide insurance cover for medication-related expenses. They have significant implications for the provision of public health care to the poor and are important for policy-makers and health management alike.

1 Introduction

"A normal delivery package is all-inclusive and includes a two-day stay, medicines, vaccinations, and a baby kit [...]." [1]

– LIFE SPRING HOSPITALS PVT LTD, HYDERABAD

"[...] after the cost of external medicines was added, the for-profit sector turned out to be cheaper than the government sector."

– WORLD BANK POLICY NOTE ON THE INDIAN HEALTH SECTOR, Radwan (2005, p.15)

The Indian private health care sector is flourishing. According to the *Economic Times*, the industry body Assocham expects medical tourism to India to become a US$2-billion per year business by 2015 (Times News Network, 2009). Foreigners come from neighbouring countries for complex surgeries that are not undertaken in their home countries, and increasing numbers are coming from developed countries, such as Europe and the United States.

While foreign patients take advantage of quick, efficient, and cheap medical procedures in highly specialised, private hospitals in Delhi, Mumbai, or Hyderabad, the urban poor in adjacent slums also turn to private health facilities. In a pilot survey of 570 micro-finance clients in urban slums in Hyderabad, we find that 63% of respondents gave birth in private hospitals, compared with only 28% in government hospitals, and 9% who delivered at home. The large proportion of people living on less than US$2 per day and who are willing to pay for health services suggests that a significant market for private health care exists in urban slums.

The purpose of this dissertation is to contribute to the resolution of a puzzle. Why do people living on less than US$2 per day choose to pay for private

---

1 http://www.lifespring.in/deliveries.html

services although public services are supposed to be available at no cost? This question applies to a range of other services such as schooling and comprises 4 billion individual answers in emerging market economies around the globe. This dissertation is on health care decisions of women in urban slums of Hyderabad, India. The narrow focus on antenatal care allows us to (1) study deliberate medical treatment choices and (2) control for a multitude of potential disease patterns.

Drawing from existing literature, we take field evidence on the availability of medicines in private and public health facilities as a starting point. Delivery packages in private hospitals to the poor, such as Hyderabad-based maternity care chain *Life Spring Ltd.*, are usually "all-inclusive", including necessary medicines and vaccinations at a fixed rate, payable up front. The situation in public hospitals is different. Here, the cost for external medication makes up for a considerable proportion of total expenses.[2] In contrast to private hospitals, expenses for medication at public hospitals is uncertain and a source of some risk.

To investigate the role of poverty on risk attitudes, we conduct Discrete Choice Experiments (DCE) with a sample of 1,227 women who are currently pregnant or have given birth within the last three years. Building on Neoclassical consumer theory and Expected Utility (EU) theory, we substantiate an explanation as to why the urban poor choose to go private: risk-aversion. Using market segmentation and market simulation studies, we derive possible health policy implications for the provision of health care to the poor.

The structure of this dissertation is as follows. Section 2 summarises the relevant literature about the privatisation of public services for the poor in general and in the Indian health sector in particular. Section 3 builds on Neoclassical consumer theory and EU theory to motivate the stated preference methodology used. Section 4 describes data, experimental design, and econometric models estimated in the empirical analysis and addresses some validity issues. The results of market segmentation and simulation studies are presented in Subsection 4.5. Section 5 concludes.

---

2 In Punjab State, the adjustment of medication makes public facilities even more expensive than private hospitals (Radwan, 2005, p. 15).

2 Literature

The phenomenon of private provision of public services, such as primary schooling and general health care, in urban slums of emerging market economies has only recently attracted the attention of scholars. Tooley and Dixon (2006), who studied private schools in India and sub-Saharan Africa, refer to this phenomenon as "de facto privatization". The authors find that these private institutions are often unrecognised by local authorities and arise because people demand them, not because of supply-side promotion of the private sector through legislation or reform.

In the Indian health care context, the private sector is expanding rapidly at the expense of the public sector. The share of private hospitalisation rose from 8% at independence in 1947, to more than 60% by the early 1990s (Radwan, 2005). The National Sample Survey 1996 reports that private agencies provide more than 70% of urban hospitalisation, while a World Bank report (Peters et al., 2001) suggests that these figures still significantly underestimate the true size of the private sector.

The growth of private service provision has mainly been attributed to poor public sector performance. More et al. (2009) find that public facilities are overcrowded, have poor sanitary standards, and lack basic drugs. Doctors are often burnt-out and pay little attention to patients' needs.

These circumstances seem to lead even those living on less than US$2 per day to resort to private health facilities. In their research on health service utilisation in Delhi, Das and Hammer (2007) found that private providers were (1) more expensive, (2) *less* qualified, and (3) more responsive to their patients' needs, both actual and *perceived*, than their public counterparts. The latter two factors result in patients spending a lot of "money for nothing" in terms of unnecessary drugs and advice. In our study, this might be reflected by an abnormally high percentage of Cesarean sections in private hospitals.[1] Das and Hammer (2007, p. 4) conclude that "the poor receive low-quality care from the private sector because doctors do not *know* much, and low-quality care from the public sector because doctors do not *do* much."

In response to these serious deficits in both public and private health service provision to the poor, academics and policy advisers stress the importance of improving the public sector provision of health services. Riley et al. (2007) argue that "unlike electric or water companies, banks, or other private businesses, health service providers have little or no economic incentive to move into slums."

However, the micro-finance industry offers a valuable lesson in business model innovations tailored to serve the poor. The industry demonstrates that market-based approaches that focus on consumer demand can be a sustainable alternative where governments fail to provide these services and private provision is suboptimal (Aghion and Morduch, 2005). Radwan (2005) makes the case for three areas of private sector activity to improve health services to the poor: (1) contracting out of health centres, (2) social franchising, and (3) demand-led financing.

Little is yet known about the demand-side of health care markets for the poor. Information about the reasons that drive their decisions for private or public health care has important implications for private and public sector actors. The identification of market segments and the poors' willingness to pay (WTP) for specific attributes of care should help private providers in formulating marketing strategies, providing the right products and charging realistic prices.

Research into the demand-side of these markets can also inform policy-makers about primary areas for improvement in public health care. This was the objective of two Discrete Choice Experiments (DCE) on rural Africa by Kruk et al. (2009a,b). They assessed the WTP for hospital attributes by women who chose to deliver at home in an effort to identify attributes that help promote

---

[1] The proportion of Cesarean sections in our sample is 49% for private hospitals. This is nearly twice as much as in public hospitals (28%) and more than three times the 15% recommended by the World Health Organization (2010).

the utilisation of existing public facilities. In rural Ethiopia, Kruk et al. (2009b) report that (1) availability of medicines and equipment, (2) professionalism of staff and (3) a receptive provider attitude were the most important hospital attributes.

Hanson et al. (2005) find the same attributes to be of importance in DCE on hospital choice in urban Zambia. They further report that the importance of both hospitalisation cost and drug availability decreases with higher socioeconomic status, i.e., wealthier respondents (1) can afford higher prices and (2) find it easier to secure private medication from external sources to fill in any gap. While the first point is obvious, the second requires interpretation. The authors suggest that the result is "probably explained by the fact that when drugs are not available they must be purchased outside the hospital, which has more negative consequences for lower socioeconomic groups" (Hanson et al., 2005, p. 698).

While the authors do not discuss this finding in more detail, they make an important point that could contribute an explanation as to why poorer households may be more inclined to choose private over public hospitals, even when private hospitals are more expensive. Field evidence shows that the costs for external medication make up a considerable proportion of hospital expenses in urban India (Radwan, 2005; More et al., 2009). The extent of these expenses is uncertain and therefore a source of some risk. A higher risk-aversion of poorer households could serve as one rational explanation as to why the poor choose to go private.

In the next section, we review the theoretical basis for the DCE methodology, which is used to test the risk-aversion hypothesis of EU theory in this context. This is intended to motivate the econometric analysis of stated preference data and facilitate the interpretation of the results in Section 4.

3 Theory

3.1 Stated preference theory

In general, preferences, if *revealed* through market behaviour are good indicators of customer preferences regarding features such as price and quality. However, Pokhrel (2006) points out that the revealed preference approach has several shortcomings when inferring preferences for health services. First, many aspects of health care are not traded in a market, as is the case with home delivery, and preferences can therefore not be inferred from market actions. Second, when comparing private and public health facilities, part of the consumption is free, or at least heavily subsidised, by either the government or private health insurance.

Contrarily, *stated* preference data can be obtained by permitting the respondent to choose between discrete alternatives. The controlled environment of the choice problem allows direct inference of preferences. The stated preference approach is relatively easy to implement and allows us to answer "what-if" questions based on market simulations. Under certain conditions, the approach gives a clear picture of the underlying preferences for attributes that determine market decisions.

A stated preference method that is particularly suited for low-literacy respondents, such as urban slum dwellers, are Discrete Choice Experiments (DCE). DCE have been widely applied in various contexts, such as marketing of new products and valuation of non-market resources, to estimate the relative importance of different attributes in the demand for goods or services (refer to Louviere et al., 2000, for an overview).

The stated preference approach is known to have strong validity in terms of convergence with other methods of preference elicitation (van der Pol et al., 2008), high external validity (Telser and Zweifel, 2007), and is known to represent actual choices better than ordinary rating or ranking exercises (Ryan et al., 2001a,b). Studies by Hanson et al. (2005) and Kruk et al. (2009a,b) suggest that pictorial depictions of attribute bundles or packages comprising different attribute levels, make DCE a viable instrument for use with illiterate respondents. Limitations of DCE are addressed together with validity issues in Section 4.

The theory underlying DCE is built upon many elements of Neoclassical consumer theory. Respondents are assumed to be rational and to maximise their utility based on a set of innate, invariate preferences. Given the traditional assumptions about the Neoclassical consumer, the discrete choice context represents an optimisation problem. The respondent adopts choices that maximise her utility, subject to her budget constraints (Ryan et al., 2008a). In what follows, three deviations from this theory that are important in the context of standard DCE and of this study are discussed.

Figure 3.1: Goods and characteristics space in Lancaster's model of consumer behaviour

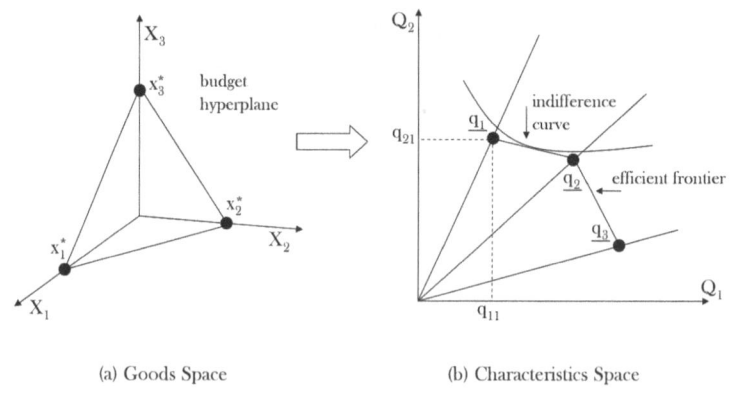

(a) Goods Space   (b) Characteristics Space

3.2 Extensions to Neoclassical consumer theory

3.2.1 Lancaster's approach

A first deviation of DCE from Neoclassical consumer theory is that we assume, based on Lancaster's (1966) approach, that it is the *attributes* of the goods that provide utility rather than the goods themselves. The relation between goods space and characteristics space is presented in Figure 3.1.

Figure 3.1a shows the budget constraint hyperplane of a choice involving goods x_1, x_2, and x_3. The polytope that is formed by the axes and the hyperplane represents a feasible region, i.e., x_j^* is the amount of good x_j, $j = 1, 2, 3$, that the consumer can afford. Consumers select that bundle of goods that maximises their utility, subject to constraints. Geometrically, if the goods are divisible, this point is where the consumer's indifference surface is tangent to the budget hyperplane.

The goods space $\mathbb{X}$ is assumed to map into characteristics space $\mathbb{Q}$ by a linear consumption technology matrix Q, with elements q_{ij} such that q_{ij} "is the quantity of the ith characteristic possessed by a unit amount of the jth good" (Lancaster, 1971, p. 15). Lancaster (1966) shows that the feasible region in $\mathbb{X}$ maps into a convex polytope in $\mathbb{Q}$, which is obtained from all convex combinations of the origin, and the vectors $\underline{q_j}$, which are the images of x_j^* in characteristics space (Figure 3.1b). In the case of divisible goods and monotonic preferences over characteristics, consumers will maximise their utility by choosing a linear combination of goods, i.e., a combination of characteristics at the point where their indifference curve is tangent to the efficient frontier of the feasible set in Figure 3.1b.

Analytically, the optimal goods combinations are obtained by solving the canonical linear programme:

$$\max_{x, d} u = u(\underline{x}, Q, d) \tag{3.1}$$

$$\text{subject to } y = p_j x_j + d. \tag{3.2}$$

The consumer chooses (x, d) so as to maximise a twice differentiable, quasi-concave, increasing utility function u defined over a vector of goods $\underline{x} =$

$[x_1, ..., x_N]^T$ and d, the numeraire or outside good. In addition, the consumer's utility depends on the $K \times N$ consumption technology matrix

$$Q = \begin{pmatrix} q_{11} & \cdots & q_{1N} \\ \vdots & \ddots & \vdots \\ q_{K1} & \cdots & q_{KN} \end{pmatrix} = (\underline{q_1}, ..., \underline{q_N}).$$

This matrix comprises the K exogenous attributes of the N non-numeraire goods, such that the jth column comprises the vector of attributes $\underline{q_j}$ of good x_j. The classical budget constraint is given in Equation (2), where y is the customer's income and p_j the price of good x_j.

3.2.2 Discrete choice

In DCE, respondents are presented with canonical *discrete* choice sets. The maximisation problem is subject to two further restrictions in addition to the budget constraint, because respondents choose among a set of (1) *fixed* and (2) *mutually exclusive* alternatives. This optimisation problem and its link to random utility models, discussed further on, was first studied by Small and Rosen (1981) and Hanemann (1982). The discussion below follows Hanemann (1982, pp. 4). The consumer now chooses (x, d) so as to maximise

$$\max_{x, d} \quad u = u(\underline{x}, Q, d) \qquad (3.1)$$

$$\text{subject to} \quad y = p_j x_j + d \qquad (3.2)$$

$$x_i x_j = 0 \quad \forall i \neq j \qquad (3.3)$$

$$x_j = \bar{x}_j \text{ or } 0. \qquad (3.4)$$

The two additional constraints (3) and (4) impose discreteness on the choice problem. Equation (3) ensures that the goods x_j are mutually exclusive in consumption and Equation (4) ensures that any one good x_j can only be purchased in some fixed quantity, $\bar{x}_j = 1$, say.

It follows directly from (3) and (4) that the consumption of good x_j is only possible as $\underline{x_j} = [0, ..., 0, \bar{x}_j, 0, ...0]^T$. For good x_1 in Figure 3.1a, the consumption vector is $\underline{x_1^*} = [1, 0, 0]^T$. From Lancaster's (1966) approach, we know that the image $\underline{q_1}$ of $\underline{x_1^*}$ in characteristics space $\mathbb{Q}$ is given by the linear transformation $\underline{q_1} = Q\underline{x_1^*}$, which is

$$q_1 = \begin{pmatrix} q_{11} & q_{12} & q_{13} \\ q_{21} & q_{22} & q_{23} \end{pmatrix} \begin{pmatrix} 1 \\ 0 \\ 0 \end{pmatrix} = \begin{pmatrix} q_{11} \\ q_{21} \end{pmatrix}.$$

Thus, the transformation from goods into characteristics space is simply given by the vector of characteristics $\underline{q_j}$ of good x_j, i.e., the jth column of the consumption technology matrix $\underline{Q}$. We find that, in the discrete choice case, only the corner solutions $\underline{q_j}$ are possible (Figure 3.1b).

Once one of the goods, e.g. x_j, has been selected, the utility – *conditional* on this decision – follows from Equations (1) to (4) and can be written as

$$\begin{aligned} u_j &= u(\bar{x}_j, \underline{q_j}, y - p_j \bar{x}_j) \\ &\equiv v_j(\underline{q_j}, y - p_j \bar{x}_j) \quad j = 1, ..., N \end{aligned}$$

where v_j is increasing in $(y - p_j \bar{x}_j)$ and the elements of $\underline{q_j}$. $v_1, ..., v_N$ are referred to as the consumer's *conditional* indirect utility functions because they are conditional on the choice of one of the N goods. The consumer's actual choices can be represented by a set of binary functions $\delta_1, ..., \delta_N$, where

$$\delta_j \equiv \begin{cases} 1 & \text{if } x_j > 0 \\ 0 & \text{if } x_j = 0. \end{cases}$$

These choices can be expressed in terms of the conditional indirect utility functions by

$$\delta_j(Q, p, y) = \begin{cases} 1 & \text{if } v_j(\underline{q_j}, y - p_j \bar{x}_j) \geq \\ & \quad v_i(\underline{q_i}, y - p_i \bar{x}_i) \; \forall i \neq j \\ 0 & \text{otherwise.} \end{cases}$$

The unconditional demand functions associated with Equations (1) to (4) can be expressed as $x_j(Q, p, y) = \delta_j(Q, p, y) \bar{x}_j$. Substitution of these demand functions into the utility function in Equation (1) yields the *unconditional indirect utility function*

$$v(Q, p, y) = max\{v_1(\underline{q_1}, y - p_1\bar{x}_1), \ldots, v_N(\underline{q_N}, y - p_N\bar{x}_N)\}.$$

$v(Q, p, y)$ measures the customer's maximised utility when confronted with given prices p, attributes Q, and income y.

3.2.3 Random utility maximization

A random utility model arises when one assumes that, although a consumer's utility function is deterministic for him, it contains some components that are unobservable to the econometric investigator and must be treated by the investigator as random variables (McFadden, 1974a). These components of the utility function may be denoted by the vector ε of i.i.d. random variables with zero means. Building on the previous results, the utility function, specialised to the binary choice between unit goods $j=1,2$, becomes

$$v(\underline{q_j}, p_j, y) + \varepsilon_j \quad j = 1, 2.$$

The consumer maximises her unconditional indirect utility function and therefore chooses good $j=1$ over good $j=2$, if her valuation for good $j=1$ exceeds that of good $j=2$, i.e. if

$$v(\underline{q_1}, y - p_1) + \varepsilon_1 \geq v(\underline{q_2}, y - p_2) + \varepsilon_2.$$

The probability that the consumer will choose the first good can therefore be written as

$$P\left\{\underbrace{v(\underline{q_1}, y - p_1) - v(\underline{q_2}, y - p_2)}_{\Delta v} \geq \underbrace{\varepsilon_2 - \varepsilon_1}_{\eta}\right\}.$$

If we specialise the utility function to a linear form, as follows:

$$v(q_j, p_j, y) = \alpha^T \underline{q_j} + \beta(y - p_j) + \varepsilon_j, \quad (3.5)$$

where $\alpha^T = [\alpha_1, ..., \alpha_K]$ is the unknown vector of coefficients of valuation related to the K levels of quality attributes in $\underline{q_j}$ and β the unknown coefficient of valuation for income, then

$$\Delta v = \alpha^T (\underline{q_1} - \underline{q_2}) - \beta(p_1 - p_2). \quad (3.6)$$

Note that the income term y cancels out due to the differencing. This property is unique to the linear utility function (Hanemann, 1984). Assuming a convenient distribution of the error term η, e.g. logistic, the probability of choosing good 1 can be modelled as binary logit with

$$P\{\Delta v \geq \eta\} = \Lambda(\Delta v),$$

where $\Lambda(\cdot)$ is the evaluation of the logistic cumulative distribution function $e^{-\Delta v}/[1 + e^{-\Delta v}]$. The resulting logit model allows for identification of the unknown vector of coefficients α and the coefficient β.

3.3 Divisible attributes

The above results and interpretation of the vector of model coefficients α hold for a "purely qualitative utility maximizing choice" (Hanemann, 1982, p. 5). However, the interpretation will be different when divisible attributes, such as medicines, are permitted. The reason is that respondents will be able to adjust the quantity of the divisible attribute, after their choice (ex post). To summarise the argument in this section, it can be shown that, if the respondent takes ex-post adjustment into account during the choice process, the model coefficient pertaining to the divisible attribute will be lower than in the case where ex post adjustment is not possible. The correct interpretation of the coefficient of the divisible attribute is therefore its valuation, *conditional* on it being part of the chosen option.

These results are derived formally below and are of ample importance for the interpretation of our empirical results, particularly for the estimated coefficients relating to the medicines component of the care package in Section 4. These results have further implications for other discrete choice situations involving divisible attributes. Apart from hospital choice, examples can be found in a variety of settings. In school choice, respondents may consider obtaining additional tutoring hours when confronted with a choice between, say, private and public schools. In tourism, respondents can usually choose between all-inclusive, half-board, breakfast only, and self-catering options, all of which include some degree of ex-post adjustment.

We now offer a formal treatment of the issue. To begin with, consider a situation where respondents are confronted with a choice between two fixed hospital care options as represented in characteristics space $\mathbb{Q}$ in Figure 3.2. In this choice context, each fixed option has two attributes, $\mathbb{Q}_{id}$ which is indivisible and $\mathbb{Q}_d$ which is divisible. One option, represented by point ID, contains a high-level $q_{id,1}$ of the indivisible attribute $\mathbb{Q}_{id}$, such as the privacy level of a ward. The other option, D, contains a high-level $q_{d,1}$ of the divisible attribute $\mathbb{Q}_d$, such as medicines. Both option D and ID are offered at price p.

Figure 3.2: Effect of ex-post adjustment

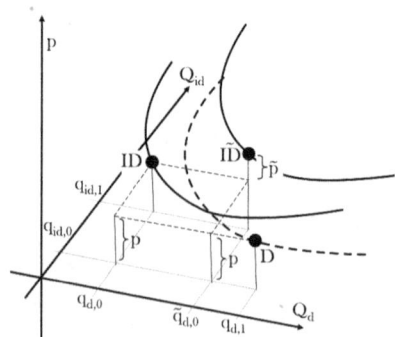

The econometric investigator observes the respondent's choice between ID and D and draws conclusions about her preferences using the stated choice model discussed above.[1] The choice of D reflects a higher utility from that choice than from ID. This means that D is on a higher utility level than ID. Let the level curve defined at price level p of the indifference surface that contains D be represented by the dashed curve. If the consumer chose D over ID, this indifference surface must be at a higher utility level than the indifference surface containing ID.

Now suppose the respondent chose ID over D. This choice can be interpreted in two ways. One interpretation would be that the indivisible attribute is valued higher than the divisible, and therefore ID is on a higher indifference surface than D, e.g. the solid curve through ID.

The choice of ID over D is also consistent with the potential for ex-post adjustment of the divisible attribute $\mathbb{Q}_d$. That is, once option ID with a lower level of the divisible attribute has been chosen, it is still possible to adjust the level of the divisible attribute by obtaining external medication $\tilde{q}_{d,0} - q_{d,0}$ for price $\tilde{p}$, say. This is equivalent to choosing point $\tilde{ID}$, which is on a level curve of the indifference surface at price level $p + \tilde{p}$.[2]

It is shown below that, as a consequence of this additional option, the probability of choosing option ID is higher when ex-post adjustment is possible. It then follows that the valuation of the divisible attribute is lower than in the case without ex-post adjustment.

We will now derive this relation analytically. Consider the choice between the two options discussed above and presented in Figure 3.2. Recall that the options differ in two attributes, and that option ID has a higher level of the indivisible attribute. The corresponding quality vector is given by

$$q_{ID} = (q_{id,1}, q_{d,0})^T = (1, 0)^T,$$

where a high level of an attribute is represented by 1 and a low level by 0. Contrarily, option D has a higher level of the divisible attribute and quality vector

---

1 The slope of indifference curves, which reflects consumer preferences, is the Marginal Rate of Substitution MRS = $\delta \alpha_i / \delta \alpha_j$ between attributes i and j.
2 Here, higher price levels indicate *lower* utility levels. Whether point C is on the same, a higher or a lower indifference surface depends on the slope of the indifference surface with respect to p.

$$\underline{q_D} = (q_{id,0}, q_{d,1})^T = (0, 1)^T.$$

A respondent will choose option ID if the following inequality holds

$$v(\underline{q_{ID}}, p, y) \geq v(\underline{q_D}, p, y)$$
$$v\left(\begin{pmatrix} q_{id,1} \\ q_{d,0} \end{pmatrix}, y - p\right) \geq v\left(\begin{pmatrix} q_{id,0} \\ q_{d,1} \end{pmatrix}, y - p\right).$$

If ex-post adjustment is possible at price $\tilde{p}$ then the respondent will choose option ID if

$$\begin{cases} v\left(\begin{pmatrix} q_{id,1} \\ q_{d,0} \end{pmatrix}, y - p\right) \geq v\left(\begin{pmatrix} q_{id,0} \\ q_{d,1} \end{pmatrix}, y - p\right) \\ v\left(\begin{pmatrix} q_{id,1} \\ \tilde{q}_{d,0} \end{pmatrix}, y - p - \tilde{p}\right) \geq v\left(\begin{pmatrix} q_{id,0} \\ q_{d,1} \end{pmatrix}, y - p\right). \end{cases}$$

The second inequality is an additional condition under which it is rational to choose ID. Therefore, as we have already seen in the graphical representation, the utility derived from choosing option ID is at least as high as in the case without ex-post adjustment.

Further, consider the linear, additive utility function from Equation (5), Section 3.2.3, with fixed price level p,

$$v(\underline{q_j}, p, y) = \alpha^T \underline{q_j} + \beta(y - p) + \varepsilon_j,$$

where $\underline{q_j} = \begin{pmatrix} q_{id} \\ q_d \end{pmatrix}_j$, the vector of quality attributes contained in option j. The difference in valuation between option D and ID then becomes

$$\begin{aligned} \Delta v &= \alpha^T(\underline{q_{ID}} - \underline{q_D}) \\ &= (\alpha_{id}, \alpha_d)\left(\begin{pmatrix} q_{id,1} \\ q_{d,0} \end{pmatrix} - \begin{pmatrix} q_{id,0} \\ q_{d,1} \end{pmatrix}\right) \\ &= (\alpha_{id}, \alpha_d)\begin{pmatrix} q_{id,1} - q_{id,0} \\ q_{d,0} - q_{d,1} \end{pmatrix} \\ &= \alpha_{id}(q_{id,1} - q_{id,0}) + \alpha_d(q_{d,0} - q_{d,1}) \\ &= \alpha_{id}(1 - 0) + \alpha_d(0 - 1) \\ &= \alpha_{id} - \alpha_d. \end{aligned} \qquad (7)$$

Option ID is chosen if $\Delta v > 0$, i.e., if the valuation of the indivisible attribute (α_{id}) is higher than the valuation of the divisible attribute (α_d). This choice occurs with probability $P(\Delta v \geq \eta)$ (Section 3.2.3).

If ex-post adjustment is possible, respondents can purchase any additional amount of the divisible attribute, for example $\tilde{q}_{d,0} - q_{d,0}$, that gives them utility $\tilde{\alpha}_d$ for price $\tilde{p}$, say. Therefore, point $\tilde{ID}$ in Figure 3.2 is a third option that provides utility $v = \alpha_{id} + \tilde{\alpha}_d + \beta(y - p - \tilde{p})$. We can rewrite the difference in valuation for the two options D and ID as $\Delta\tilde{v}$, the maximum of Δv in the case without (Equation 7), and with, ex-post adjustment

$$\Delta\tilde{v} = max\{\alpha_{id} - \alpha_d,\ \alpha_{id} + \underbrace{\tilde{\alpha}_d - \beta\tilde{p}}_{ex-post\ adj.} - \alpha_d\}.$$

If ex-post adjustment is possible, option ID is chosen if $\Delta\tilde{v} \geq 0$. Note that we find $P(\Delta\tilde{v} \geq \eta) \geq P(\Delta v \geq \eta)$, i.e., if ex-post adjustment is possible, the consumer is at least as likely to choose ID as in the standard case without ex-post adjustment. The above relation can be rewritten as:

$$\begin{aligned}\Delta\tilde{v} &= max\{\alpha_{id} - \alpha_d,\ \alpha_{id} - \alpha_d + \underbrace{\tilde{\alpha}_d - \beta\tilde{p}}_{ex-post\ adj.}\}\\ &= \alpha_{id} - \alpha_d + max\{0,\ \tilde{\alpha}_d - \beta\tilde{p}\}\\ &= \underbrace{\alpha_{id} + max\{0,\ \tilde{\alpha}_d - \beta\tilde{p}\}}_{Choice\ of\ ID} - \underbrace{\alpha_d}_{Choice\ of\ D}.\\ &= \alpha_{id} - \underbrace{\left[\alpha_d - max\{0,\ \tilde{\alpha}_d - \beta\tilde{p}\}\right]}_{conditional\ value\ of\ \alpha_d\ =:\ \alpha_{d|D}}.\end{aligned}$$

To see that the term in square brackets ($\alpha_{d|D}$) is the valuation of the divisible attribute, *conditional* on having it in the hospital package, consider the term as the difference between the unconditional valuation (α_d) and the valuation of adjusting a required amount ex post $max\{0,\ \tilde{\alpha}_d - \beta\tilde{p}\}$, which is $\alpha_{d|ID}$. Obviously, ex-post adjustment is only considered if it yields utility larger zero, i.e., $\tilde{\alpha}_d > \beta\tilde{p}$.

We therefore need to adjust the interpretation of the coefficient that pertains to the divisible attribute. The relevant econometric estimate is not to be interpreted as the valuation of medicines but rather as the valuation of obtaining medicines as part of the hospital package, instead of having to adjust it ex-post. This distinction will be useful for the interpretation of the results in Section 4.

3.4 Choice under uncertainty

The fourth and final extension to Neoclassical consumer theory is to allow for uncertainty about the amount of the divisible attribute that may be needed. Obtaining a guarantee of a higher level of medication with the hospital package can be seen as insurance against uncertain expenses for external medication.

Neoclassical consumer theory treats insurance as a normal good that is characterised by a positive income elasticity of demand. However, due to the uncertainty about consumer's future health status, it is not utility but expected utility that is maximised. Arguably the most popular theory that pertains to decisions under uncertainty is the von Neumann and Morgenstern Expected Utility (EU) theory. The EU hypothesis asserts that the demand for insurance is the choice between an uncertain and a certain loss (von Neumann and Morgenstern, 1944). Consumers are risk-averse in the sense that they exhibit a concave utility function in income, as illustrated in Figure 3.3.

Figure 3.3: Risk averse utility function

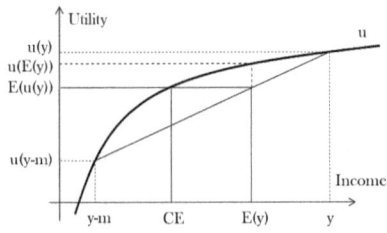

Now consider the necessity to obtain external medication ex post as an uncertain event that has a probability distribution over the interval $[y - m, y]$, where y is the consumer's initial income and m the cost of external medication in case it is needed. The associated expected income is $E(y)$. Under EU, consumers are expected utility maximisers. A risk-neutral consumer, whose utility function would be a linear combination of the best scenario at point $(y, u(y))$ and the worst scenario at point $(y - m, u(y - m))$, would be indifferent between uncertain external medical expenses and certain expenses of $y - E(y)$. Her certainty equivalent is $E(y)$. A risk-averse expected utility maximising consumer, however, has a lower certainty equivalent of CE, due to her concave utility function. She would be willing to pay a risk premium $E(y) - CE$.

The link between EU theory and stated preference theory is the certainty equivalent. The CE is the valuation of having medication as part of the hospital package, which is $\alpha_{d|D}$. Because of the concavity of their utility function, more risk-averse respondents are willing to pay a higher risk premium, i.e., have a higher valuation for obtaining medication directly with the hospital package.

To find an answer to the initial question of whether risk-aversion plays a role in poor patients' decisions to go private, we need to find the relation between income and risk-aversion. EU theory is quiet on this issue. Though theories exist to model this relation, the question whether the poor are more likely to privately insure themselves is an empirical one.[3] In the following Section 4, we estimate the relation between income, risk-aversion, and insurance demand empirically.

---

3 Refer to Schneider (2004) for a comprehensive literature review.

4 Empirical Analysis

4.1 Data

The data for this study were collected in August through October 2009 by five interviewers. The study area comprised 65 slums with an estimated total population of 115,000 in the four divisions Kukatpally, L.B. Nagar, Mehdipatnam, and Tarnaka of the city of Hyderabad. The samples were drawn to represent the estimated population of each of the slums. The interviewers identified potential respondents at their homes in the study area and conducted personal interviews with those women who were then pregnant or had given birth in the previous three years.

Respondents were interviewed about their revealed and stated preferences for maternity services. Preferences revealed through market behaviour were categorised into whether respondents had chosen home delivery, a public, or a private hospital for their most recent delivery. Stated preferences were elicited using DCE with pictorial depictions of hypothetical hospital packages in several choice cards, presented further on (Figure 4.1). In addition to hospital choice, respondents were interviewed about predisposing, enabling, and need factors based on the Andersen (1995) model of health service utilisation. The framework has been applied in both industrialised and emerging market economies to explain the utilisation of health services.[1] It distinguishes three factors that determine health service utilisation: predisposing, enabling, and need factors. Questionnaire I for women who had given birth in the previous 3 years, and Questionnaire II for women who were pregnant for the first time, can both be found in Annex D. We realised a sample of 1,227 respondents, of which we used 1,107 responses for the final analysis.

---

[1] Choi (2006); Chou and Chi (2004); Forbes and Janzen (2004); Suci (2006); Sunil et al. (2006); Trinh et al. (2007); Varenne et al. (2006)

Figure 4.1: Sample choice cards

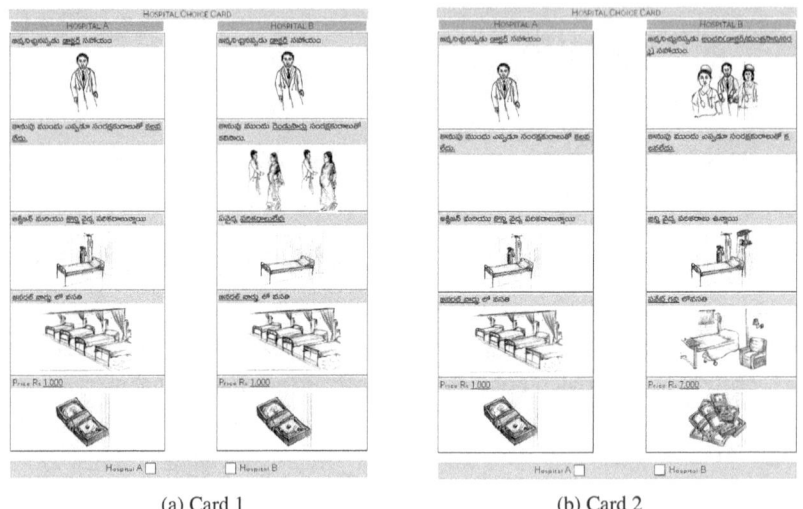

(a) Card 1   (b) Card 2

4.2 Survey design

In a first step, we identified important quality attributes in hospital choice through a pilot survey with 570 micro-finance clients in slums of Hyderabad, who were pregnant or had given birth in the last three years. We categorised quality aspects into five attribute groups, following the literature review in Burge et al. (2005). In addition to *price*, we distinguished between two attributes describing quality of care

- *Professionalism of staff*
  levels: midwife; doctor; team comprising doctor and midwives

- *Continuity of care*
  levels: never meet the team; meet once; meet twice

and two attributes representing quality of the facility

- *Availability of medicines and equipment*
  levels: no medicines and equipment; medium availability; full availability

- *Privacy of room*
  levels: general ward; shared room; private room.

These attributes were pretested in focus-group discussions with micro-finance clients and translated into Hindi and the local languages Telugu and Urdu. For the graphical depiction of these attribute levels used in the study, please refer to Figure 5.1 in Annex A.

In the main survey, 1,227 respondents in 65 slums of Hyderabad were presented with binary choice problems. In the choice problem, the respondent was offered the choice between two hypothetical maternity service packages, each comprising a specific combination of different levels of the five attributes. The attribute "availability of *medicines and equipment*" was made up of the following three levels. "Low" which represents only basic drugs for sanitation. The "medium" level offers anaesthetic gas for pain relief and basic medication and vaccinations for mother and child. "Full" medicines and equipment availability comprises the "all inclusive" package including care for postnatal complications and, if required, transfer to a specialised hospital.

Given the levels of the five attributes, one of which is price, respondents were asked to choose one service package in paired comparisons. The choice involves a trade-off between different aspects of health care. Two sample choice cards are presented in Figure 4.1 to illustrate the choice task. SPSS Orthoplan procedure was employed to generate a fractional factorial design of 49 cards, of which 14 were dropped because they were either (weakly) dominated by, or (weakly) dominate the constant scenario "Hospital A". The constant scenario is present as the first hospital package in all choice cards (Figure 4.1) and used as the reference category in the econometric analysis. The remaining 35 cards were split into four choice sets and randomised across respondents so that every respondent had to make a maximum of nine and a minimum of eight pairwise comparisons.

4.3 Econometric model

4.3.1 Binary choice model

Respondents' utility functions are modeled using the random utility model (McFadden, 1974a). Following Lancaster's (1966) consumer theory, patients' choices are explained by the difference in hospital attribute levels present in options Hospital A and Hospital B (Figure 4.1). As option Hospital A is fixed for all choice cards, respondents' preferences can simply be determined by the presence or absence of attribute levels in option Hospital B.

The binary choice problem is modeled by the latent variable model

$$u^*_{ijk} = \mathbb{X}_{ijk}\beta + \varepsilon_{ijk}, \qquad (4.1)$$

where $\mathbb{X}_{ijk}$ is a vector representing the attribute levels in choice card $i=1,...,n_j$ from choice set $j=1,...,4$, shown to respondent $k=1,...,1107$, where the number of choice cards per set is $n_1=8$ and $n_j=9$ for $j > 1$. The columns of the design matrix $\mathbb{X}$ comprise an intercept and the 5 attribute factors. To allow for identifiability of the coefficient vector β, we use corner point constraints. Coefficient estimates are therefore defined as differences from the reference category present in option Hospital A, which is called the "corner point" (Barnett and Dobson, 2008, p. 39). The dependent variable u^*_{ijk} is a latent variable defined as

$$u_{ijk} = \begin{cases} 1 & \text{if } u^*_{ijk} > 0 \\ 0 & \text{if } u^*_{ijk} \leq 0, \end{cases}$$

where $u_{ijk} = 1$ indicates the kth respondent's choice of hospital option 'Hospital B' in choice card i in choice set j. Choices are explained by the respondents' preferences captured by the 11×1 coefficient vector β and the hospital choice cards given their attribute levels represented by the $9,757 \times 11$ design matrix $\mathbb{X}$.

The estimated coefficients pertaining to each attribute level represent logistically transformed utility points for different attribute levels. The fraction β_m/β_n of two coefficients can therefore be interpreted as marginal rate of substitution between two hospital attributes m and n. The Willingness To Pay (WTP) estimate for attribute level m is obtained by the ratio $-\beta_m/\beta_{price}$.

4.3.2 Bayesian hierarchical logit

To allow for preferences of the same respondent to be correlated across different choice problems, the model is extended to a random coefficients model

$$u^*_{ijk} = \mathbb{X}_{ijk}(\beta + \eta_k) + \varepsilon_{ijk}, \qquad (4.2)$$

where observations are modelled as random draws ε_{ijk} from a Bernoulli distribution plus additional draws η_k from a normal distribution for each individual k's attribute coefficients (Train, 2003). η_k is a normally distributed, respondent-specific error term that models correlation of repeated choices by the same respondent and preference heterogeneity between them.

Reformulating the random coefficients mo-del with a second equation

$$\eta_k = \Gamma s_l + \zeta_k, \qquad (4.3)$$

specifies a hierarchical logit model (Rossi et al., 2005) that helps to explain preference heterogeneity η_k across respondents, i.e., how preferences differ by sociodemographic groups s_l. In Equation (10), Γ is a matrix of coefficients that relate η_k to the value of sociodemographics s_l of sociodemographic group l. Specifically, the (m, n)-th entry relates the valuation of attribute m to the value of covariate n. The sociodemographic covariates s_l used in the analysis are based on the well-established Andersen (1995) behavioural model of health service utilisation. Finally, $\zeta_k \sim i.i.d.N(0, \Sigma)$ is the unobserved heterogeneity component that is assumed to follow an i.i.d. normal distribution with mean 0 and covariance matrix Σ. In the absence of Γs_l, Equation (10) specifies the standard random-coefficients distribution.

The model is estimated using Markov Chain Monte Carlo (MCMC) methods implemented in the statistical software package *bayesm* (Rossi and McCulloch, 2005) in the *R* environment (please refer to Annex C for the script).

4.4 Validity issues

4.4.1 Lexicographic preferences

An important assumption in DCE is that respondents are willing to trade amongst attributes in the choice set. It is literally impossible to make inferences about the utility functions of respondents who are unwilling to trade, because it is then not possible to estimate their marginal rates of substitution between attribute levels. Including such respondents can lead to a misspecification of the regression model due to violation of the independence of irrelevant alternatives (IIA) assumption. This leads to misinterpretation of the results and erroneous conclusions (Ryan and Skåtun, 2003). Therefore, the first validity issue we need to address before we estimate or interpret the results is potential non-trading behaviour, also known as lexicographic preferences.

There are two main reasons for non-trading behaviour. The first is the respondent's unwillingness or inability to choose a package that contains any payment above a certain threshold. A second reason is that respondents may apply heuristics to simplify the choice task. Testing for lexicographic preferences is therefore of ample importance when researching the choice behaviour of low-income and low-literacy respondents.

Such a test has to build upon the fact that lexicographic preference structures entail stepwise decision-making. In the first step, respondents may focus on a small number of attributes before they consider other attributes in step two. A concept that is closely related to this choice process is that of dominant preferences. Dominant preferences with respect to the price attribute would imply that, confronted with any two options, the respondent will *always* choose the cheaper one. Cairns et al. (2002), McIntosh and Ryan (2002), and Scott (2002) employ the existence of dominant preferences to infer the presence of lexicographic preference orderings.

However, the observation of dominant preferences is not sufficient by itself to infer non-trading behaviour. Gryd-Hansen and Skjoldborg (2008) suggest two alternative explanations that would lead to these preference patterns being observed. First, dominant preferences may be an artefact of the experimental design. Respondents who are unwilling to trade attributes in the current design,

Table 4.1: Tests for lexicographic preferences

Panel A: Test Results by Household Income:

$\hat{\beta}^{full}$	$\hat{\beta}^{reduced}$	$\hat{\sigma}_{\hat{\beta}^{full}-\hat{\beta}^{reduced}}$	T	p-value	Income Group	Sample Size
0.71***	0.37***	0.06	5.39	0.00	>5,000	529
0.71***	0.46***	0.08	3.31	0.00	3,000-5,000	357
0.72***	0.61***	0.11	0.93	0.18	≤3,000	221

Significance codes: 0 '***' 0.01 '**' 0.05 '*' 0.1 ' ' 1

Panel B: Test Results by Literacy Status:

$\hat{\beta}^{full}$	$\hat{\beta}^{reduced}$	$\hat{\sigma}_{\hat{\beta}^{full}-\hat{\beta}^{reduced}}$	T	p-value	Literacy Status	Sample Size
0.79***	0.45***	0.08	4.08	0.00	Illiterate	311

Significance codes: 0 '***' 0.01 '**' 0.05 '*' 0.1 ' ' 1

may well do so when presented with other designs. Second, it is impossible for the econometric investigator to account for respondents having different thresholds – for example price thresholds – for trading/non-trading behaviour by simply observing their choices.

Gryd-Hansen and Skjoldborg (2008) therefore propose a two-stage test procedure for lexicographic preferences that is based on the step-wise decision-making process underlying lexicographic preferences. In the first stage, the full choice model is estimated and the price coefficient $\hat{\beta}_{price}^{full}$ and its variance $\hat{\sigma}_{\beta_{price}^{full}}^{2}$ are obtained. In a second step, all other choice attributes except the price attribute are dropped from the model and again we obtain $\hat{\beta}_{price}^{reduced}$ and $\hat{\sigma}_{\beta_{price}^{reduced}}^{2}$. The test statistic

$$T = \frac{\hat{\beta}_{price}^{full} - \hat{\beta}_{price}^{reduced}}{\sqrt{\hat{\sigma}_{\beta_{price}^{full}}^{2} + \hat{\sigma}_{\beta_{price}^{reduced}}^{2}}} \sim t$$

follows a t-distribution.

The logic behind the test is as follows. If some trading takes place between price and other attributes, dropping other attributes would affect the estimate of the price coefficient. The reason is that the relation between choice and price is more poorly explained in this case and therefore the variance σ^2 of the random error ε should increase. In choice models, the coefficients are scaled by the factor $1/\sigma$. Therefore, the coefficient $\hat{\beta}_{price}^{reduced}$ is expected to be significantly lower than $\hat{\beta}_{price}^{full}$ when trading takes place, relative to the case when respondents are unwilling to trade.

The results of this test for lexicographic preferences by income and by literacy status are presented in Table 4.1. The low t-value of 0.93 (Panel A, Row 3) suggests that non-trading behaviour with respect to price is a problem for the low-income group with a mon-thly income of less than Rs 3,000. The reason seems to be their tight budget. The application of heuristics to simplify the choice task seems less likely. Such a strategy would be especially appealing for low-literacy respondents. However, we find that non-trading behaviour is not an issue for them (t-value: 4.08, Panel B). While there is obviously some overlap between illiterate and low-income respondents (Table 4.2), their choice behaviours are distinct.

Table 4.2: Two-way table of relative frequencies by income and literacy status

	Household Income	
	$> Rs\ 3{,}000$	$\leq Rs\ 3{,}000$
Literate	0.59	0.13
Illiterate	0.21	0.07

Non-trading behaviour is mainly, but not solely, related to the price attribute (Gryd-Hansen and Skjoldborg, 2008). However, price is the most important choice attribute throughout all socioeconomic groups and it appears natural to test lexicographic preferences for the price attribute. Further tests, which are not reported here, suggest that non-trading behaviour is not an issue for the remaining four attributes.

In order to overcome the issue of lexicographic preference orderings, the literature takes two directions. The more traditional approach is to employ additional survey questions, for example by asking respondents which attributes they paid attention to (Hensher, 2008). More recent approaches try to incorporate non-trading behaviour in the statistical models that are used to derive the welfare estimates. Scarpa et al. (2009) for example, use latent class logit models to estimate the probability of each respondent having lexicographic preferences. These probabilities are used in a second model to condition the attribute values in a multinomial error-component logit model. While this might be a valuable robustness check for our results, we proceed, noting that the t-test is rather conservative in that it does not take into account the fact that the variances are obtained from the same sample.

4.4.2 Further validity issues

There are six further sources of bias we need to address before we continue. A first, potential issue in statistical surveys is *non-response bias*. While we found most respondents very keen to take the survey and express their opinion,

Muslim women were an exception. During the field surveys in Muslim areas, we found women withdrawn into purdha and unwilling to participate in the survey.

A second validity issue is *hypothetical bias*. As respondents do not back up their choice with real commitments they may respond differently from how they would choose in reality. The resulting theoretical bias is a well-studied disadvantage of stated preference methods (List and Shogren, 1998). We believe that we bypassed this bias to some degree by explicitly linking respondents' choices to actual hospital packages to be provided by Hyderabad-based micro-lender Spandana.

Third, to identify those who do not appear to understand the technique or are not taking it seriously (Ryan, 1999), we conduct tests of (theoretical) validity and consistency. Internal validity is tested by comparing estimated coefficients in the market segmentation study with a priori expectations. Internal consistency was checked by testing the rationality of choices made: 86 out of the original 1,227 observations that violated the rationality or transitivity of preferences assumption were removed from the sample.

Fourth, though we conducted the survey with women only, decision-making in health care is a joint process. In our sample, only 9% of women make health-related decisions on their own. In 54% of cases studied, the place of delivery is jointly decided upon by the married couple, 26% of respondents said their husbands would make the decision for them, and 11% stated that the decision was made by others in the household or the family. While we forgo modelling these interdependencies here, they should be taken into consideration by future studies on this clientele.

A fifth validity issue we need to address is the assumption of additive utility functions. This assumption neglects possible interaction effects between attribute levels. For example, it is reasonable to assume a higher frequency of consultation to lead to a higher increase in utility if the medical caregiver is a doctor than if it is a midwife. These two attributes are complements. They are "clustered", in that higher levels of both consistently appear together. The fractional factorial design used in this study offers limited scope for tests of interaction effects. Athey and Stern (1998) provide an econometric test procedure for complementarity, based on unobservables, that could prove useful in this context and should be considered in future research using fractional factorial designs in DCE.

A final issue is that our WTP estimates are essentially unconditional, because we did not include a "choose neither" or opt-out option. However, there are good reasons not to include an opt-out option in this choice scenario. Unlike most consumer goods, respondents do have to choose one or another place of delivery so that an opt-out option seems infeasible. Further, including an opt-out option is subject to bias itself (Bennett and Blamey, 2001). Respondents may misuse it to avoid making difficult decisions. Further, allowing for opt-out options reduces the information on respondents' preferences in hypothetical alternatives. Opt-out options also create econometric challenges. If respondents choose the opt-out option, it is unclear where they would deliver instead and how this choice is to be modelled. To prevent the problem of misinterpreting unconditional WTP estimates, we (1) used Hospital A as a constant scenario in all choice cards to avoid forcing respondents to pay more than they are able or willing to pay, and (2) refer our WTP estimates to actual hospital expenditures.

4.5 Results

4.5.1 Market segmentation

The estimates of the Bayesian Hierarchical Logit model are presented in Table 5.1, Annex B. The first row gives the incremental WTP estimate for an attribute level compared to the reference category (given in brackets). As discussed in the model part, the WTP estimates for attribute level m are obtained by the ratio β_m/β_{price}. Due to the definition of price as a factor, we obtain two coefficient estimates for price. For the calculation of WTP, we use the coefficient that gives the decrease in utility due to an increase in price from the reference level of Rs 1,000 to Rs 6,000. The entry in row 1, column 2 in Table 5.1

reads as follows. When increasing the package price by Rs 6,000, the average respondent wants to be compensated with Rs 6,000.[2]

For an increase in *medicines and equipment*, from medium to full medicines, respondents are willing to pay an additional Rs 5,248 on average. Interestingly, a change in degree of *privacy* from general ward to private room only increases WTP by Rs 1,532, compared to an increase of Rs 1,886 for a change to a shared room. The provision of private rooms therefore clearly does not make economic sense for the *average* respondent. However, note that there may well be a market segment that prefers a private room over a shared room and is willing to pay for it.

To rank the importance of hospital attri-butes, we compare the range of utility points – transformed into monetary units – of the five attributes. The WTP analysis shows that, while availability of *medicines and equipment* has the largest range of WTP estimates (Rs 9,620 for full compared to low medicines), the span of *continuity* of care is the second widest. Indeed, attention by medical staff is one of the most underprovided attributes in the Indian context. In Das and Hammer's (2007) study, doctors in Delhi spend 3.8 minutes on a consultation and ask three questions on average. Without any prior diagnostics, this is all the attention a patient can expect to get.

The deviation from the mean for different sociodemographic groups – categorised by Andersen's (1995) model – is given in subsequent rows.[3] For example, to obtain the average WTP for illiterate respondents, we would add the estimates in the third row in Table 5.1 to the mean WTP estimate in the first row.

Predisposing factors, the first category in the Andersen (1995) model of health service utilisation, give a mixed picture.

- Muslims, who make up 34% of respondents, are very *price* sensitive. For an increase in package price by Rs 3,000, ceteris paribus, they

---

2 Respondents would then accept a compensation of Rs 1,847 for an increase in price by Rs 3,000 on average. This is a result of respondents' underlying, non-linear utility function (Figure 4.2). From the *law of diminishing marginal utility*, we know that each rupee one pays is more "painful" than the previous rupee.

3 In the Hierarchical Bayes Regression, sociodemographic variables were mean-centred. Estimates can therefore be interpreted as deviation from the mean in the first row.

require Rs 828 more compensation than the average respondent; for a Rs 6,000 price change for the packages, Muslims' WTP estimates deviate downwards from the average by Rs 802.

- In line with common expectation, respondents living in larger households are *price* sensitive at the expense of *privacy* of room. Those women who belong to communities that value homebirth, also value *privacy* of room, at the expense of *medicines and equipment*. And those who have their first antenatal check-up in later stages of their pregnancy, attach less importance to *continuity* of care.

Table 4.3: Correlation matrix of individual-level part-worths

	Price	Privacy	Prof.	Medicines
Privacy	-0.637***			
Prof.	-0.007	-0.111**		
Medicines	0.582***	-0.486***	-0.309***	
Continuity	-0.434***	0.133**	0.823***	-0.666***

Significance codes: 0 '***' 0.01 '**' 0.05 '*' 0.1 ' ' 1
Number of Observations: 1,107

The two remaining factors in Andersen's (1995) model give a very clear preference structure.

- Factors *enabling* the utilisation of health services, such as a higher income and financial support by the family, are associated with lower price sensitivity, i.e., WTP measures of these respondents significantly exceed those of the average respondent in all health care attributes. While poorer households exhibit a lower WTP for insurance, they are willing to pay a higher fraction of their household income on this full medicines option. This finding is consistent with Dror et al. (2007), who study the WTP for general health insurance in India using a bidding game.

- *Need* factors, such as complications in respondents' current or previous pregnancy or birth by Cesarean section, are linked with strong preferences for *professionalism* of medical staff.

A further approach to segment the market is to identify clusters of customers based on their preferences. The group-specific WTP estimates (in Table 5.1, Annex B) allow us to derive individual-level preferences by adding the relevant group-specific WTP to the mean estimate in the first row.[4]

A first step is the analysis of inter-attribute correlations. From the first column in Table 4.3, we find that respondents trade off price against quality attributes, as expected. Price-sensitive respondents attach less value to *privacy* ($\rho=-0.637$), *continuity* of care ($\rho=-0.434$) – both significant at the 99% confidence level – and *professionalism* ($\rho=-0.007$). However, the valuation for availability of *medicines and equipment* ($\rho=0.582$) significantly increases with price sensitivity. The positive correlation suggests that price-sensitive respondents find it least attractive to have to obtain external medication. This points to a higher demand for insurance by price-sensitive respondents.[5] The following subsection will investigate this demand structure in detail and discuss potential reasons behind it.

4.5.2 Insurance demand of the poor

In the following, we investigate the insurance demand, which could be one of the variables that determines the poors' choice of private hospitals. In a second step, we test the risk-aversion hypothesis that, according to EU theory, could be a possible reason for insurance demand.

To get a clear picture of the demand for insurance by income groups, we use our WTP estimates from Table 5.1 and calculate part-worths of each attribute level for the three income groups. The part-worth is a heuristic measure to determine the percentage contribution of a certain attribute level to the

---

[4] Instead of a model with dummy variables, we use continuous attribute definitions that impose a linear utility function on respondents' preferences. This model allows for a straightforward interpretation of entries in the parsimonious 5x5 correlation matrix in Table 4.3.

[5] Under the reasonable assumption that the provision of medication by a private hospital is not cheaper than obtaining it from a pharmacy.

Table 4.4: Part-worths

from: to:	Δ Price		Δ Medicines & Equipment			Δ Continuity			Σ
	Rs 1,000 Rs 4,000	Rs 4,000 Rs 7,000	Low Medium	Medium Full		Never meet Meet once	Meet once Meet twice		
Mean	-0.07	-0.16	0.17	0.20		0.13	0.08		0.81
Low Income	-0.08	-0.21	0.13	0.24		0.12	0.14		0.92
Medium	-0.07	-0.14	0.18	0.19		0.14	0.05		0.77
High	-0.07	-0.14	0.18	0.19		0.13	0.08		0.79
Low/Medium	1.09	1.47	0.72	1.23		0.90	2.49		–
Low/High	1.20	1.46	0.74	1.25		0.97	1.80		–

Number of Observations: 1,107

choice decision (Weitz and Wensley, 2002, p. 197). It is defined as a fraction. The numerator is the WTP estimate for the level at hand with respect to the immediate lower level. The denominator is the sum of the *ranges* in WTP for all five attributes. The resulting part-worth for the attribute level is in the interval [0;1]. In our case, equal importance of all five attributes in the choice decision would result in part-worths of $1/(2*5)=0.1$.

Table 4.4 gives part-worths for the three most important attributes. Together, these three attributes make up for 81% of the total range of WTP. For the low-income group, these attributes explain as much as 92% of variation in WTP. The part-worth of full medi-cines for the average respondent (0.2) is obtained by dividing the WTP for full as compared to medium medicines (Rs 5,248 in Table 5.1, Row 1, Column 8) by the sum of ranges of all five attributes.[6]

A comparison of part-worth for *medicines and equipment* for different income groups, ceteris paribus, shows that the poor attach more importance to full medication (0.24) than higher income groups (0.19) (Table 4.4, Column 4). The ratio of these metrics is given in the last two rows as 1.23 and 1.25 respectively. Interestingly, the high-income groups attach more value (0.18) to medium versus no medicines than the poor (0.13). This has two rationales. First, high-income-groups may find it easier to adjust medicines (medium to full), but they may consider the non-existence of any type of medicines and equipment a signal of poor overall quality. Second, low-income groups may value the first step change from no to medium medicines less than the subsequent step change, because the first step is a more or less certain expense, while the latter contains more uncertainty.

The latter point brings us to the issue of risk-aversion of the poor. As discussed in the theory part in Section 3, risk-aversion is directly reflected in the utility function. Figure 4.2 shows the utility functions in residual income (*income - price*) for the three income groups, based on the Hierarchical Bayes estimates in Table 5.1. Given the piece-wise linear form of the utility functions, concavity

---

6 This sum of ranges is obtained from the first row in Table 5.1 and given by Rs 6,000 (*Price*) + Rs 1,886 (*Privacy*) + Rs 2,972 (=1,908+1,064) (*Professionalism*) + Rs 9,620 (=4,372+5,248) (*Equipment*) + Rs 5,592 (*Continuity*).

can be measured using the inner angles of the three utility representations. As can be seen in Figure 4.2, the angle for the low-income group (153°) is significantly lower than the 160° and 158° for the other income groups. This suggests that EU theory offers a partial explanation for insurance choice in this context: risk-aversion.[7]

Figure 4.2: Utility functions by income

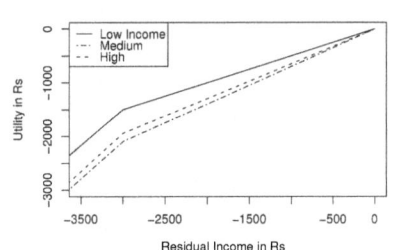

There are at least two theories that explain the higher risk-aversion of low-income groups. *State-dependent utility theory* suggests that consumers' insurance demands are dependent on their state, such as their health and socioeconomic status (Anscombe and Aumann, 1963). According to this theory, it is the anticipated need for medical care – given the current state – that determines the insurance demand. Anticipating the greater health risks that result from impoverished living conditions, low-income consumers are expected to have a higher degree of risk-aversion. In contrast, *poverty literature* mainly focusses on risk-aversion and time preferences of the poor. Wagstaff (2000) points out that households are expected to become increasingly risk-averse as they move closer to poverty, because every drop in income can push them below the survival point. However, the poor might still choose not to insure, as they may have to choose present over future consumption out of necessity.

---

7 An extension to the descriptive analysis above would be a statistical test for significant differences in risk-aversion. Modelling the price attribute as orthogonal polynomial of degree two in the Hierarchical Bayes Regression, allows us to test for significant differences in the 2nd order coefficients of the three income groups. Finding these differences then allows us to reject the null hypothesis of equal risk-aversion.

4.5.3 Market simulations

In the above subsection, we identified availability of medicines and equipment as one possible determinant that leads the poor to opt for private hospitals out of an insurance motive. It may be recalled from the introductory section that a key difference between public and private hospitals is that public facilities require patients to get external medication, whereas private hospitals offer pre-specified "all-inclusive" care packages.

An important policy issue is the estimation of the positive effect that availability of medication could have on the market share of the public sector. As such an effect would not come without costs, a second question concerns consumers' willingness to pay for this improvement. Answers to both these questions are important for policy makers and health management alike. The individual-level preferences elicited with DCE allow us to conduct market simulations to obtain estimates of both these effects.

In the first step to approaching these questions, we define four hypothetical maternity care packages that represent hospital "competition" in the market simulation. We used expert judgement of two doctors and one hospital administrator to define these packages. The rows in Table 4.5 represent (A) home birth and (B) government hospital, both priced at Rs 1,000, as well as two private options, (C) and (D), priced at Rs 7,000. Option A comprises the lowest levels of professionalism and medicines but high levels of privacy and continuity, representing a homebirth scenario. Option B offers medium levels of professionalism and medicines, but provides little privacy and continuity, representing a government hospital scenario. The private options are made up of two categories. C provides full *medicines and equipment*, representing the "insured package", while D dominates C in all other attributes, but provides medium *medicines and equipment* only.

The market share of these options are calculated with (1) 1st choice rule and (2) Logit rule (Table 4.5, Columns 6 & 7). The so-called *1st choice rule* assumes respondents opt for the product that provides the most utility. This decision rule clearly overstates respondents' choice probability by mapping the choice probability of the package with the highest choice probability to 1.

Table 4.5: Hospital options for simulation and simulated market share

			Attribute Levels			Simulated Market Share	
	Price	Privacy	Prof.	Medicines	Continuity	1st Choice	Logit Rule
A: Home Birth	1000	Private	Nurse	Low	Twice	3.16%	3.31%
B: Govt Hospital	1000	General	Doctor	Medium	Once	60.07%	56.94%
C: Private I	7000	General	Doctor	Full	Once	18.88%	22.05%
D: Private II	7000	Private	Team	Medium	Twice	17.89%	17.70%

Number of Observations: 1,107

However, it may be more realistic when considering deliberate choices such as place of delivery. The formal notation is as follows

$$p_{k,s|S}^{(1st)} = \begin{cases} 1 & \text{if } \mathbb{X}_s^S(\beta + \eta_k) \geq \mathbb{X}_{s'}^S(\beta + \eta_k) \\ & \forall s' \in S \\ 0 & \text{otherwise.} \end{cases}$$

That is, we assume respondent k chooses the hospital package containing attribute levels $s \in S$ if the utility score of this option, given by the linear predictor $\mathbb{X}_s^S(\beta + \eta_k)$ from the regression model (Equation 9), is higher than $s' \in S$ for all subsets s' of S.

The *Logit rule* satisfies the probabilistic nature of choices but results crucially hinge on the IIA (independence of irrelevant alternatives) assumption (Schwaiger and Opitz, 2003). That is, we implicitly assume that relative choice probabilities of other market options do not change upon exclusion of one alternative. Using the famous example of transportational choice with red and blue buses, McFadden (1974b) shows that this assumption is not likely to hold if market alternatives are similar. The formal definition of the Logit rule is

$$p_{k,s|S}^{logit} = \frac{exp\{\mathbb{X}_s^S(\beta + \eta_k)\}}{\sum_{s' \in S} exp\{\mathbb{X}_{s'}^S(\beta + \eta_k)\}}.$$

That is, respondent k's log-odds of choosing the hospital option containing attribute levels $s \in S$ are given by the linear predictor $\mathbb{X}_s^S(\beta + \eta_k)$ from the regression model in Equation (9).

As can be seen in Table 4.5, columns 6 and 7, both decision rules result in quite similar estimates of market shares. To test for the validity of the expert opinion, we compare market shares and attribute levels of the simulation with the survey data about actual hospital choices.

The simulated *market shares* are consistent with real market shares for home birth (5%), government (46%), and private hospital (49%) based on our sample of 1,227 respondents. Regarding *attribute levels*, the price for private hospital options (Rs 7,000) is in line with the median price (Rs 8,000) paid in private hospitals by low-risk patients having a non-Cesarean delivery.

Women who gave birth in government facilities and at home report that they paid a maximum of Rs 1,000 but are often required to buy additional drugs not available at their facility. The median total costs for a low-risk, non-Cesarean delivery for home birth and government hospital are Rs 3,000 and Rs 4,000, respectively.

Based on this set of packages in the market and their market shares, we can now conduct market simulations to (1) determine potential changes in market shares and (2) derive WTP estimates for any proposed change in attribute levels of government hospitals. The simulation is conducted repeating the following steps for each of the attributes, taking the government hospital option B as the base option.

Figure 4.3: Policy simulation for option "Govt Hospital"

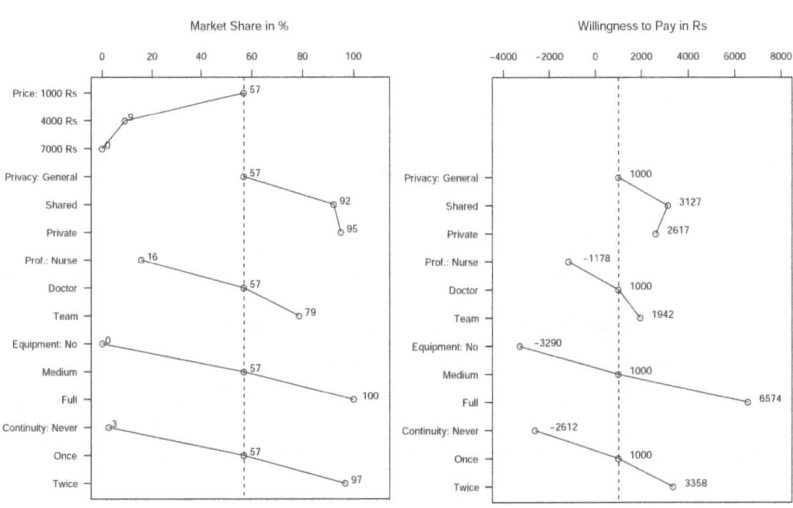

(a) Market share of option "Govt Hospital" (b) Willingness to pay for variations of "Govt Hospital"

- First, the base case is simulated with packages A through D placed in competition with one another. The market share of the government hospital (B) obtained by Logit rule (56.94%) is given in Table 4.5,

41

Column 7. This market share is the baseline plotted on the dashed, vertical line in Figure 4.3a.

- Second, another simulation is conducted in which the base option B is modified by changing one attribute level at a time (holding the competing packages A, C, and D constant). The share of preference for B (the government hospital option) increases from 57% to 100% if we manage to offer full medicines instead of medium medicines, ceteris paribus (Figure 4.3a).

- Finally, additional simulations are performed raising the price of the new package B (the base package but now with full medicines) until its market share again drops to the original 57% (holding competition constant). A price increase from Rs 1,000 (original government package) to Rs 6,574 is needed to come back to the original market share of 57% (Figure 4.3b). The difference in price (Rs 5,574) between the modified package B (with full medicines and equipment at higher price) that captures 57%, and the original base package B that captured 57%, reflects the market WTP for the package upgrade – given the competitive context and the objective of maintaining constant market share.

The simulated WTP for full medicines and equipment as compared to the 'medium' level base package (6,574 - 1,000 = Rs 5,574) exceeds the WTP of Rs 5,248 derived for the average respondent (Table 5.1, Annex B). This suggests that those respondents who, according to their preference structure, are most likely to choose the government hospital option are willing to pay an additional Rs 326 for the insurance package, compared to the average respondent.

Overall, the simulation results for the government hospital option are similar to the regression results in Table 5.1, Annex B. The most important attributes, based on WTP range in Figure 4.3b, are availability of *medicines and equipment* and *continuity* of care. Also in line with regression results, the WTP for an upgrade to a shared room (Rs 2,127) is higher than that for an upgrade to a private room (Rs 1,617). However, the *market share* of the government hospital option increases by 3% (=95%-92%) if it includes a private room instead of a shared room. This observation is a result of the hospital competition introduced in the simulation. A large proportion of those respondents who originally preferred the home birth option (which includes a private room) only switch to the government hospital if a private room is provided there as well. However, these respondents are the first to switch back to the home birth option, as we progressively increase the price in the simulation to determine the WTP for the upgraded government hospital option. This explains the lower WTP value for private rooms. While there is sufficient demand for private rooms, as reflected in a higher market share, those demanding it have lower purchasing power (lower WTP) than those preferring a shared room.

The simulation results are important for policymakers and health management for two main reasons. First, they suggest that the *simulated* market share of public hospitals can be significantly increased by either of two main improvements: improved supply of medicines and equipment (increase up to 100%) or improvements in the continuity of provider attention (97%). Second, the results provide a WTP estimate of Rs 5,574 for a full medical insurance package for those respondents who are most likely to choose a government hospital.

The natural trade-off between price and market share allows for the determination of appropriate price levels that will realise policy objectives. For example, a price of Rs 5,574 for the insurance package leaves the market share of the government hospital unchanged at 57%. Any drop in price increases the market share. A considerable drop even leads to a *simulated* market share of up to 100%.

5 Conclusion

This dissertation is a first stated preference study of the demand-side of the burgeoning maternity care market in urban Indian slums. The study contributes three major insights to inform the current debate on private provision of health services to the poor.

First, we show that Discrete Choice Experiments (DCE) are a viable tool to assess demand in bottom of the pyramid markets with large proportions (28%) of illiterates. In fact, 93% of respondents passed the tests for rationality and transitivity of preferences. Nonetheless, there are two issues in DCE in BoP markets that are worth pointing out for future research. One issue that is dominant in DCE with low-income and illiterate respondents are lexicographic preference orderings. Asking respondents to think aloud while taking the questionnaire, as proposed in a recent study by Ryan et al. (2008b), could prove useful in identifying lexicographic preference orderings and circumvent associated estimation problems. Another issue is joint decision-making in health-related choices. We find that only 9% of the respondents make health-related decisions on their own. Modelling joint decisions, as shown in Rossi et al. (2005), would improve external validity of estimates.

Second, in line with previous DCE on hospital choice in developing countries, we find that availability of *medicines and equipment* and *continuity of care* are the most important hospital attributes. The market segmentation shows that the lowest income group attaches more value to an upgrade from a medium to a full medication package, compared to higher income groups. The poor patients' part-worths derived from medium medication alone are, however, lower than that of more affluent respondents. This preference pattern indicates a higher insurance demand for medication by the lowest income group. In line with expected utility theory, we provide empirical evidence that this insurance demand of the poor is partially explained by their risk-aversion.

The main contribution of this dissertation is to link these findings with field evidence on availability of medicines in private and public hospitals. While patients in public hospitals often have to get external medication, private hospitals offer pre-specified care packages that include a full medication component. This allows us to determine one key explanation as to why the urban poor choose private over public hospitals: risk-aversion with respect to medical expenses.

Using market simulations, we show that the provision of a full medication component can improve the (simulated) market share of the public sector in slums of Hyderabad from the current 57% to up to 100%. Our findings suggest that, instead of spending too much on efforts to provide free basic medication, an effective pro-poor policy for public hospitals could be to let patients pay for basic drugs but insure high expenses for medication.

Bibliography

Aghion, B. and Morduch, J. (2005). *The Economics of Microfinance*. MIT Press.

Andersen, R. (1995). Revisiting the Behavioural Model and Access to Medical Care: Does it Matter? *Journal of Health and Social Behaviour*, 36(1):1–10.

Anscombe, F. and Aumann, R. (1963). A Definition of Subjective Probability. *Annals of Mathematical Statistics*, 43:199âĂŞ–205.

Athey, S. and Stern, S. (1998). An Empirical Framework for Testing Theories About Complementarity in Organizational Design. Working paper, National Bureau of Economic Research.

Barnett, A. and Dobson, A. (2008). *An Introduction to Generalized Linear Models*. Chapman & Hall, CRC.

Bennett, J. and Blamey, R. (2001). *The Choice Modelling Approach to Environmental Valuation*. Edward Elgar Publishing.

Burge, P., Devlin, N., Appleby, J., Rohr, C., and Grant, J. (2005). London Patient Choice Project Evaluation: A model of patientsâĂŹ choices of hospital from stated and revealed preference choice data. Technical report, RAND Europe.

Cairns, J., Van Der Pol, M., and Lloyd, A. (2002). Decision Making Heuristics and the Elicitation of Preferences: Being fast and frugal about the future. *Health Economics*, 11(7):655–658.

Choi, S. (2006). Insurance Status and Health Service Utilization Among Newly-arrived Older Immigrants. *Journal of Immigrant and Minority Health*, 8(2):149–161.

Chou, K. and Chi, I. (2004). Factors Associated with the Use of Publicly Funded Services by Hong Kong Chinese Older Adults. *Social Science & Medicine*, 58(6):1025–1035.

Das, J. and Hammer, J. (2007). Money for Nothing: The Dire Straits of Medical Practice in Delhi, India. *Journal of Development Economics*, 83(1):1–36.

Dror, D., Radermacher, R., and Koren, R. (2007). Willingness to Pay for Health Insurance Among Rural and Poor Persons: Field evidence from seven micro health insurance units in India. *Health Policy*, 82(1):12–27.

Forbes, D. and Janzen, B. (2004). Comparison of Rural and Urban Users and Non-users of Home Care in Canada. *Canadian Journal of Rural Medicine*, 9(4):227–35.

Gryd-Hansen, D. and Skjoldborg, U. (2008). *Using Discrete Choice Experiments to Value Health and Health Care*, chapter The Price Proxy in Discrete Choice Experiments: Issues of relevance for future research, pages 175–193. Springer.

Hanemann, W. (1982). Applied Welfare Analysis with Qualitative Response Models. Working Paper 241, University of California, Berkeley.

Hanemann, W. (1984). Welfare Evaluations in Contingent Valuation Experiments with Discrete Responses. *American journal of Agricultural Economics*, 66(3):332–341.

Hanson, K., McPake, B., Nakamba, P., and Archard, L. (2005). Preferences for Hospital Quality in Zambia: Results from a Discrete Choice Experiment. *Health Economics*, 14(7):687–702.

Hensher, D. (2008). Joint Estimation of Process and Outcome in Choice Experiments and Implications for Willingness to Pay. *Journal of Transport Economics and Policy*, 42(2):297–322.

Kruk, M., Paczkowski, M., Mbaruku, G., de Pinho, H., and Galea, S. (2009a). Women's Preferences for Place of Delivery in Rural Tanzania: A Population-Based Discrete Choice Experiment. *American Journal of Public Health*, 99(9):1666–1672.

Kruk, M., Paczkowski, M., Tegegn, A., Tessema, F., Hadley, C., Asefa, M., and Galea, S. (2009b). Women's Preferences for Obstetric Care in Rural Ethiopia: a Population-based Discrete Choice Experiment in a Region With Low Rates of Facility Delivery. *Journal of Epidemiol Community Health*.

Lancaster, K. (1966). A New Approach to Consumer Theory. *The Journal of Political Economy*, 74(2):132–157.

Lancaster, K. (1971). *Consumer Demand: A new approach*. Columbia University Press.

List, J. and Shogren, J. (1998). Experimental Calibration of the Difference Between Actual and Hypothetical Reported Valuations. *Journal of Economic Behavior and Organization*, 37(2):193–205.

Louviere, J., Hensher, D., and Swait, J. (2000). *Stated Choice Methods: Analysis and Applications.* Cambridge University Press.

McFadden, D. (1974a). *Frontiers in Econometrics*, chapter Conditional Logit Analysis of Qualitative Choice Behavior, pages 105–142. Academic Press: New York.

McFadden, D. (1974b). The Measurement of Urban Travel Demand. *Journal of Public Economics*, 3(4):303–328.

McIntosh, E. and Ryan, M. (2002). Using Discrete Choice Experiments to Derive Welfare Estimates for the Provision of Elective Surgery: Implications of discontinuous preferences. *Journal of Economic Psychology*, 23(3):367–382.

More, N., Bapat, U., Das, S., Barnett, S., Costello, A., Fernandez, A., and Osrin, D. (2009). Inequalities in Maternity Care and Newborn Outcomes: One-Year Surveillance of Births in Vulnerable Slum Communities in Mumbai. *International Journal for Equity in Health*, 8(1):21–31.

Peters, D., Yazbeck, A., Sharma, R., Ramana, G., Pritchett, L., and Wagstaff, A. (2001). *Raising the Sights: Better health systems for Indiaâ̌Zs poor.* The World Bank.

Pokhrel, S. (2006). Scaling up Health Interventions in Resource-poor Countries: What Role Does Research in Stated-preference Framework Play? *Health Research Policy Systems*, 4(1):4.

Radwan, I. (2005). India - Private Health Services for the Poor: A Policy Note. Discussion Paper, The World Bank.

Riley, L., Ko, A., Unger, A., and Reis, M. (2007). Slum Health: Diseases of Neglected Populations. *BMC International Health and Human Rights*, 7(1):2.

Rossi, P., Allenby, G., and McCulloch, R. (2005). *Bayesian Statistics and Marketing*. Wiley & Sons.

Rossi, P. and McCulloch, R. (2005). Bayesm: Bayesian Inference for Marketing/Microeconometrics. *R Package Version*.

Ryan, M. (1999). Using Conjoint Analysis to take Account of Patient Preferences and go Beyond Health Outcomes: An Application to In Vitro Fertilisation. *Social Science & Medicine*, 48(4):535–546.

Ryan, M., Bate, A., Eastmond, C., and Ludbrook, A. (2001a). Use of Discrete Choice Experiments to Elicit Preferences. *Quality in Health Care*, 10(1):i55.

Ryan, M., Gerard, K., and Amaya-Amaya, M. (2008a). *Using Discrete Choice Experiments to Value Health and Health Care*, chapter Discrete Choice Experiments in a Nutshell, pages 13–46. Springer.

Ryan, M., Scott, D., Reeves, C., Bate, A., Van Teijlingen, E., Russell, E., Napper, M., and Robb, C. (2001b). Eliciting Public Preferences for Healthcare: A systematic review of techniques. *Health Technology Assessment (Winchester, England)*, 5(5):1.

Ryan, M. and Skåtun, D. (2003). Modelling Non-demanders in Choice Experiments. *Health Economics*, 13(4):397–402.

Ryan, M., Watson, V., and Entwistle, V. (2008b). Rationalising the âĂŸIrrationalâĂŹ: A think aloud study of discrete choice experiment responses. *Health Economics*, 18(3):321–336.

Scarpa, R., Gilbride, T., Campbell, D., and Hensher, D. (2009). Modelling attribute non-attendance in choice experiments for rural landscape valuation. *European Review of Agricultural Economics*, 36(24):151–174.

Schneider, P. (2004). Why Should the Poor Insure? Theories of Decision-making in the Context of Health Insurance. *Health Policy and Planning*, 19(6):349–355.

Schwaiger, M. and Opitz, O., editors (2003). *Exploratory Data Analysis in Empirical Research*, volume XVI of *Proceedings of the 25th Annual Conference of the Gesellschaft für Klassifikation*. University of Munich, Berlin: Springer.

Scott, A. (2002). Identifying and Analysing Dominant Preferences in Discrete Choice Experiments: An application in health care. *Journal of Economic Psychology*, 23(3):383–398.

Small, K. and Rosen, H. (1981). Applied Welfare Economics with Discrete Choice Models. *Econometrica*, 49(1):105–130.

Suci, E. (2006). Child Access to Health Services During the Economic Crisis: An Indonesian experience of the safety net program. *Social Science & Medicine*, 63(11):2912–2925.

Sunil, T., Rajaram, S., and Zottarelli, L. (2006). Do Individual and Program Factors Matter in the Utilization of Maternal Care Services in Rural India? A theoretical approach. *Social Science & Medicine*, 62(8):1943–1957.

Telser, H. and Zweifel, P. (2007). Validity of Discrete Choice Experiments. Evidence for health risk reduction. *Applied Economics*, 39(1):69–78.

Times News Network (2009). Indian Medical Tourism to Touch Rs 9,500 Crore by 2015: Assocham. *The Economic Times, India*, 6 January 2009.

Tooley, J. and Dixon, P. (2006). "De facto" Privatisation of Education and the Poor: Implications of a Study from Sub-Saharan Africa and India. *Compare: A Journal of Comparative Education*, 36(4):20.

Train, K. (2003). *Discrete Choice Methods with Simulation*. Cambridge University Press.

Trinh, L., Dibley, M., and Byles, J. (2007). Determinants of Antenatal Care Utilization in Three Rural Areas of Vietnam. *Public Health Nursing*, 24(4):300.

van der Pol, M., Shiell, A., Au, F., Johnston, D., and Tough, S. (2008). Convergent Validity Between a Discrete Choice Experiment and a Direct, Open-ended Method: Comparison of preferred attribute levels and willingness to pay estimates. *Social Science & Medicine*, 67(12):2043–2050.

Varenne, B., Petersen, P., Fournet, F., Msellati, P., Gary, J., Ouattara, S., Harang, M., and Salem, G. (2006). Illness-related Behaviour and Utilization of Oral Health Services Among Adult City-dwellers in Burkina Faso: evidence from a household survey. *BMC Health Services Research*, 6(1):164.

von Neumann, J. and Morgenstern, O. (1944). *Theory of Games and Economic Behavior*. Princeton University Press.

Wagstaff, A. (2000). Research on Equity, Poverty, and Health: Lessons for the developing world. Technical report, The World Bank.

Weitz, B. and Wensley, R. (2002). *Handbook of Marketing*. Sage Publications.

World Health Organization (2010). Method of Delivery and Pregnancy Outcomes in Asia: The WHO Global Survey on Maternal and Perinatal Health 2007-08. *The Lancet*, 375:490–499.

Annex A: Reference Card

Figure 5.1: Reference card

ATTRIBUTES	LEVELS		
Price ధర	రూ॥ 1,000	రూ॥ 4,000	రూ॥ 7,000
	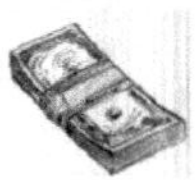	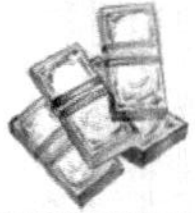	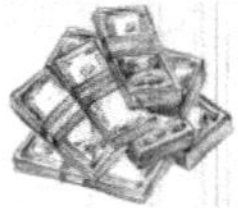
Privacy of room స్వేచ్ఛా వసతి	జనరల్ వార్డు లో వసతి	షేర్‌రూమ్ లో వసతి	ప్రైవేట్ గది లోవసతి
	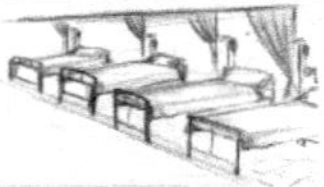	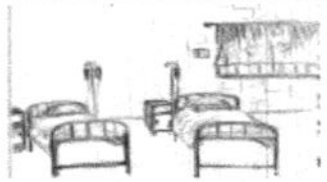	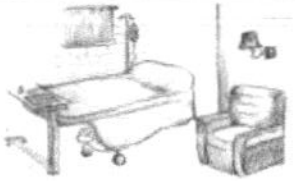
Professionalism of staff ఉన్నత వృత్తి నిర్వాహకులు	జన్మనిచ్చునప్పుడు మంత్రసాని/నర్సు సహాయం	జన్మనిచ్చినప్పుడు డాక్టర్ సహాయం	జన్మనిచ్చునప్పుడు అందరి(డాక్టర్/మంత్రసాని/నర్సు) సహాయం.
	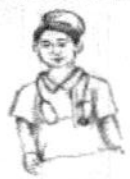	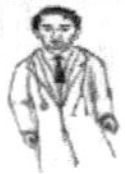	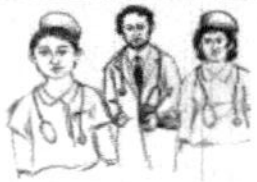
Quality of med. Equipment వైద్యపరికరాల నాణ్యత	ఏవైద్య పరికరాలులేవు	ఆక్సిజన్ మరియు కొన్ని వైద్య పరికరాలున్నాయి	అన్ని వైద్య పరికరాలు ఉన్నాయి
	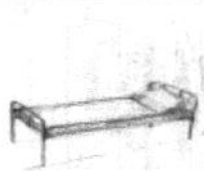	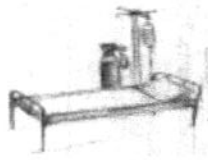	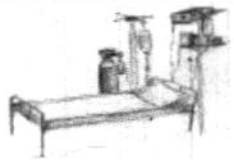
Continuity of care నిరంతర సంరక్షణ	కానుపు ముందు ఎప్పుడూ సంరక్షకురాలు తో కలవలేదు.	కానుపు ముందు ఒకసారి సంరక్షకురాలుతో కలిసారు.	కానుపు ముందు రెండుసార్లు సంరక్షకురాలు తో కలిసారు.
		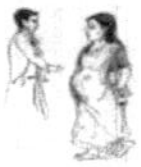	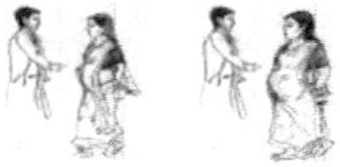

Annex B: Regression Results

Table 5.1: Willingness to pay (in Rs) by demographics for discrete attribute levels

	Price (Ref: Rs 1000)		Privacy (Ref: General Ward)		Professionalism (Ref: Doctor)		Medicines & Equipment (Ref: Medium)		Continuity (Ref: Never met)	
	Rs 4000	Rs 7000	Shared	Private	Nurse	Team	Low	Full	Once	Twice
Mean	-1847***	-6000***	1886***	1532***	-1908***	1064***	-4372***	5248***	3434***	5592***
Predisposing Factors										
No. of Children	-9	-409*	-212	-171	108	74	-513**	-152	315	-121
Illiterate	-108	-452*	-183	-189	-644**	-179	-320	406*	437*	65
Muslim	-828***	-802***	164	344	38	-286	454*	-224	-62	-22
Household-size	-408*	-37	-409*	-6	-18	347	133	252	180	-59
Value to Homebirth	-1104***	-85	279	745***	129	135	680**	67	-269	-225
First month Antenatal Care	44	-265	-104	-58	636**	472*	-978***	-151	-588**	-327
Enabling Factors										
Income Rs 3,000 - 5,000	-250	-272	909***	160	-483*	157	-971***	361*	636**	84
Income > Rs 5,000	-97	-220	579**	321	-390*	735***	-885***	367*	406*	501**
Family Finance	-203	-61	495**	-104	316	204	-186	-51	186	-193
Need Factors										
Health at Risk	89	-237	-483*	103	-254	246	-254	-56	292	339
Birth by Cesarean	-321	-457*	-376*	-366*	249	521**	420*	76	40	-262

Significance codes: 0 '***' 0.01 '**' 0.05 '*' 0.1 ' ' 1
Number of Observations: 9,757

Annex C: R Script

```
#-------------------------------------------------------------------------------
#--- Reading & Organizing Data for Bayesian Hierachical Model --------------

# mean-center data so that mean of the random effects
# distribution can be interpreted as the average respondent's
# part-worths

Z<-Z2
Z[,1]<-rep(1,nrow(Z))
dim(Z)
for(i in 2:19) Z[,i]<-Z[,i] - mean(Z[,i])
Z<-as.matrix(Z)

# Form data list for each respondent that contains their choice vector (y_h)
# and matrix of attribute descriptors (X_h) whose lengths correspond to the
# number of responses:

# First, identify the unique respondent indicators (hh)
# and determine the number of respondents (nhh) in the study.
hh<-levels(factor(choiceAtt[,1]))
nhh<-length(hh)

# Second, generate list of zero length.
lgtdata<-NULL

# Third, execute the following loop. At the end of the loop, the variable
# Data contains 946 elements, with each containing the respondent's data.
for(i in 1:nhh){
  y<-choiceAtt[choiceAtt[,1]==hh[i],2]
  nobs<-length(y)
  X<-as.matrix(choiceAtt[choiceAtt[,1]==hh[i],c(3:7)])
  lgtdata[[i]]<-list(y=y,X=X)
}

# Read data in R
Data<-list(lgtdata=lgtdata,Z=Z)


# List of parameters that control the Markov Chain
# R:       number of iterations
# sbeta: step size of the Metropolis-Hastings random-walk chain
# keep:   every xth step is kept and other draws are discarded from analysis
Mcmc<-list(R=20000,sbeta=0.2,keep=20)
```

```
# The first element of Data is comprised of two variables, y and X:
Data$lgtdata[[1]]

# write comments to screen to monitor progress
library(bayesm)
cat("Finished Reading data",fill=TRUE)
fsh()

# Call subroutine to execute MCMC computations
out<-rhierBinLogit(Data=Data,Mcmc=Mcmc)


#-----------------------------------------------------------------------
#--- Obtaining Parameter Estimates -------------------------------------

# plot grand means of random effects distribution (first row of Delta)
index<-4*c(0:11)+1
par(mfrow=c(1,1))
matplot(out$Deltadraw[,index],type="l",xlab="Iterations/20",ylab="",
  main="Average Respondent Part-Worths")

# plot of the diagonal elements of the covariance matrix:
index<-c(0:11)*15+1 # why 15?
matplot(out$Vbetadraw[,index],type="l",xlab="Iterations/20",ylab="",
  main="V-beta Draws")

# plot of log-likelihood values that are useful for assessing model fit:
plot(out$llike, type="l", xlab="Iterations/20",ylab=" ",
  main="Posterior Log Likelihood")

# plot of the rejection rate of the Metropolis-Hastings algorithm:
plot(out$reject,type="l",xlab="Iterations/20",ylab=" ",
  main="Rejection Rate of the Metropolis-Hastings Algorithm")

# Distribution of heterogeneity for selected part-worths using draws
# of the individual respondent part-worths \beta_h
# (posterior distribution of heterogeneity)
par(mfrow=c(3,4))
plot(density(out$betadraw[,1,500:1000]), main="Price.4000")
plot(density(out$betadraw[,2,500:1000]), main="Price.7000")
plot(density(out$betadraw[,3,500:1000]), main="Privacy.Shared")
plot(density(out$betadraw[,4,500:1000]), main="Privacy.Private")
plot(density(out$betadraw[,5,500:1000]), main="Professionalism.Nurse")
plot(density(out$betadraw[,6,500:1000]), main="Professionalism.Team")
plot(density(out$betadraw[,7,500:1000]), main="Medication.No")
plot(density(out$betadraw[,8,500:1000]), main="Medication.Full")
plot(density(out$betadraw[,9,500:1000]), main="Continuity.Once")
plot(density(out$betadraw[,10,500:1000]), main="Continuity.Twice")

# Estimates of the individual-level posterior distributions for one
# respondent (No. 250).
```

```
plot(density(out$betadraw[250,1,500:1000]), main="Medium Fixed Interest",
  xlab=" ",xlim=c(-15,15),ylim=c(0,.35))

# Point estimates of the means of the coefficient matrix Delta
# generated from saved draws
matrix(apply(out$Vbetadraw[500:1000,],2,mean),ncol=10)

# Point estimates of the standard deviations of the coefficient matrix
matrix(apply(out$Vbetadraw[500:1000,],2,sd),ncol=10)
```

Annex D: Survey Questionnaires

Spandana Maternity Care Market Research Study
- Cover Sheet –

Respondents Name _____ Contact Number _____

[1] Interviewer Name: _____ [2] Interviewer ID: _____ [3] Area: _____ [4] Slum: _____

Choice of Questionnaire

[5] Have you given birth in the last <u>three</u> years (i.e. after July 2006)? ☐ YES Questionnaire I
గత 3 సం॥లలో మీరు జన్మనిచ్చారా? ☐ NO Question [6]

[6] Are you pregnant now? [Symptom: missed menstrual period] ☐ YES Questionnaire II
ప్రస్తుతం మీరు గర్భవతులా? ☐ NO Quit

Questions regarding Hospital Choice Card

[7] Please rank the importance of the five attributes (price, privacy of room, Professionalism of staff, quality of equipment, continuity of care) from <u>1 (most important)</u> to <u>5 (least important)</u>. Please refer to the <u>reference card</u> when making your choice.
దయచేసి క్రింది వాటిలో అతిముఖ్యమైన అంశాన్ని "1" నుంచి తక్కువ ముఖ్యమైన దానికి "5"ను రాంక్ చేయండి. రిఫరెన్స్ కార్డ్ చూసి దీని సమాధానం ఇవ్వండి.

RANK	ATTRIBUTE	
☐	Price	ధర
☐	Privacy of room	స్వేచ్ఛా వసతి
☐	Professionalism of staff	ఉన్నత వృత్తి నిర్వాహకులు
☐	Quality of equipment	పరికరాల నాణ్యత
☐	Continuity of care	నిరంతర సంరక్షణ

[8] Please refer to the 11 hospital choice cards. On each card, the 5 pictures on the left and the 5 pictures on the right represent one hospital care package. We are interested in your preference for either Hospital A to the left **or** Hospital B to the right. To make the task easier for you, we kept Hospital A as a constant scenario. In case you do not understand one or both of the options please feel free to ask me.
హాస్పిటల్ కార్డును చూసి ప్రతికార్డుపై 5 బొమ్మలు కుడి మరియు ఎడమ ఒక్కొక్క హాస్పిటల్ కేర్ ప్యాకేజ్ ఉంది. మీ ప్రాముఖ్యత తెలుసుకునేందుకు హాస్పిటల్ "ఎ" ప్రతిసాలి ఒకటీ ఉంచాము. దయచేసి ఒకటి ఎన్నుకోండి.

☐ Choice Set 1   ☐ Choice Set 2   ☐ Choice Set 3   ☐ Choice Set 4

Choice Card	Hospital Choice	
	A	B
1	☐	☐
2	☐	☐
3	☐	☐
4	☐	☐
5	☐	☐
6	☐	☐
7	☐	☐
8	☐	☐
9	☐	☐
10	☐	☐
11	☐	☐

Comments of Interviewer: _____
_____

Spandana Maternity Care Market Research Study
- Questionnaire I for women who have given birth in the last 3 years -

[9] What name was given to your most recent live-birth?
ఈ మధ్య కాలంలో మీరు జన్మనిచ్చు బిడ్డకు ఏ పేరు పెట్టారు ?

_____ (=NAME)

Interviewer: I would first like to ask you some questions about your person.
మొదటగా వ్యక్తిగత విషయాలు, మీ గురించి కొన్ని ప్రశ్నలు అడగతోరుచున్నాము.

[10] What was your age when you gave birth to (NAME)?
మీకు ---------(పేరు) పుట్టినప్పుడు మీ వయస్సు ఎంత?

_____ years

[11] What is the highest educational institution you have attended successfully?
మీరు ఉత్తీర్ణులయిన ఉన్నత విద్య ఏది?

☐ Illiterate ☐ Can read but no schooling ☐ 3. Standard ☐ 4.-6. Standard ☐ 7.-10. Standard ☐ College, no graduate ☐ Graduate

[12] What is the highest educational institution (NAME)'s father has attended successfully?
గీి గార్గ తండ్రి ఏ ఉన్నత విద్య లో ఉత్తీర్ణులయ్యారు?

☐ Illiterate ☐ Can read but no schooling ☐ 3. Standard ☐ 4.-6. Standard ☐ 7.-10. Standard ☐ College, no graduate ☐ Graduate

[13] Were you member of a Self-Help Group (SHG) in a micro-finance program, chit fund, ROSCA or any similar group lending and saving schemes during your pregnancy with (NAME)?
మీరు గర్భవతులయినప్పుడు మైక్రోఫైనాన్స్ ప్రోగ్రామ్లో సెల్ఫ్గ్రూప్ (స్వీయ సహాయ సంస్థ) నందు, చిట్ ఫండ్, ROSCA (రొస్కా) సభ్యత్వం కలదా? ఏదైనా చిన్న మొత్తాల పొదుపు మరియు అప్పుల సంస్థల యందు సభ్యత్వం కలదా?

☐ Yes ☐ No

[14] What is your religion? మీ మతము ఏది?

☐ Hindu ☐ Muslim ☐ Christian ☐ Sikh ☐ Other ☐ None

[15] Do you belong to a scheduled caste, a scheduled tribe, other backward class, or none of these?
మీరు షెడ్యూల్ కాస్ట్/ ట్రైబ్ లేక ఇతర వెనుకబడిన తరగతికి చెందుతారా?

☐ Scheduled caste ☐ Scheduled tribe ☐ Other Backward Class ☐ None of these

[16] Does your community value giving birth at home?
మీ కులంలో ఇంటిలో ప్రసవించే ప్రాముఖ్యత ఉందా?

☐ Yes ☐ No

[17] Did the majority of your ___ deliver in health facilities?
మీ కుటుంబ సభ్యులలో అధిక సంఖ్యలో ఆరోగ్యకేంద్రాలలో ప్రసవించారా?

family members / relatives		☐ Yes	☐ No
friends		☐ Yes	☐ No
Self-Help Group/Chit/ROSCA members	☐ Not Applicable	☐ Yes	☐ No

Interviewer: Now I would like to ask you some questions about your economic situation.
ఇప్పుడు మీ యొక్క ఆర్థిక స్థోమత స్థితిగతులు అడగతోరుచున్నాము?

[18] What is your household income in Rs per month?
మీ కుటుంబ ఆర్థిక రాబడి మొత్తం నెలకి ఎంత?

☐ <1500 Rs.   ☐ 1500-3000   ☐ 3001-5000   ☐ 5001-8000   ☐ >8000

[19] What is the number of people living in your household?
మీ కుటుంబ సభ్యులు మొత్తం ఎంత మంది?

_____ people

[20] Do you / does your household own land or housing?
మీకు సొంత ఇల్లు లేక భూములు ఉన్నాయా?

☐ Yes ☐ No

[21] <u>If you / your household owns housing:</u> What is your roof made of?
మీ ఇంటి కప్పు దేనితో నిర్మించబడినది?

☐ Thatch   ☐ Tiles   ☐ Sheets   ☐ Slab   ☐ Not Applicable

[22] Does your household have the following items?
ఈ క్రింది వాటిలో మీ ఇంట్లో ఉన్న వస్తువులు ఏమిటి ?

☐ Pressure cookers   ☐ FAN   ☐ Television   ☐ Scooter/motorcycle   ☐ Almirah/Dressing table

[23] In your household, who is the main decision-maker in health related issues?
మీ కుటుంబంలో ఆరోగ్య విషయంలో ఎవరు ముఖ్య సలహాదారులు?

☐ Me   ☐ Husband   ☐ Me & husband jointly   ☐ Others in household   ☐ Others in family   ☐ Others

Interviewer: The following are questions about your pregnancy with (NAME).
ఈ క్రింది ప్రశ్నలు మీ యొక్క (పేరు) గర్భధారణను గురించినవి

[24] Did you receive antenatal care (check-up) for the pregnancy with (NAME)?
మీరు --------- తో గర్భం ధరించునప్పుడు చికిత్స లభించిందా ?

☐ Yes   ☐ No

[25] <u>If you received antenatal care at least once:</u> How many times did you receive antenatal care during this pregnancy? మీ గర్భ సమయంలో ఎన్నిసార్లు చికిత్స లభించింది?

Number of times : _____   ☐ Not Applicable

[26] <u>If you received antenatal care at least once:</u> How many months pregnant were you when you first received antenatal care for this pregnancy? మీరు మొదటిసారి గర్భచికిత్స చేసినప్పుడు ఎన్నేళ్లు ?

Number of Months: _____   ☐ Not Applicable

[27] Financial source for delivery ప్రసవం చేయటానికి తగిన ఆదాయం ఏది ?

☐ Savings ☐ Funding from family/ in-laws ☐ Bank loan ☐ SHG loan/ Chit/ ROSCA ☐ Health/ Employer's insurance ☐ Other: (specify) _____

[28] What is the travel-distance from your home to the closest health facility of the respective sectors that provides maternity services?
మీ ఇంటినుంచి సమీపంగా ఉన్న ప్రసూతిసేవలు కల్గిఉన్న ఆరోగ్యసంస్థల యొక్క ప్రయాణ దూరం ఎంత?

Govt. hospital distance: _____ km   Pvt. hospital distance: _____ km

[29] What were the total costs of your delivery of (NAME) in Rs (antenatal care fees, scans, medicines, transport and delivery costs)? మీరు ప్రసవ సమయం వరకు వెచ్చించిన మొత్తం ఎంత?

_____ Rs.

Interviewer: Finally, I would like to ask you six questions about your baby and potential complications during pregnancy.
చివరిగా మీబిడ్డ గురించి మరియు గర్భం దరించినప్పుడు ఏమైనా ఎదుర్కొన్న సమస్యలు గురించి అడగకోరుచున్నాము?

[30] Do you have relatives or friends that had a stillbirth or complications during their pregnancy?
మీ యొక్క బంధువులలో లేక స్నేహితులలో గర్భం నశించిపోవుట లేక గర్భదారణ సమయంలో సమస్యలు ఎదుర్కొన్నారా?

☐ Yes   ☐ No

[31] Where did you give birth to (NAME)? మీరు ఏ స్థలంలో ప్రసవించారు?

☐ at home   ☐ Govt. hosp.   ☐ Pvt. hospital   ☐ Other: _____ (specify)

[32] To how many children have you given birth, excluding (NAME)?
మీరు ఎంతమంది పిల్లలకు జన్మనిచ్చారు?

_____ children

[33] <u>If at least one:</u> To how many sons have you given birth, excluding (NAME)?
మీరు ఎంతమంది మగ పిల్లలకు జన్మనిచ్చారు?

_____ sons   ☐ Not Applicable

[34] Was (NAME) given birth by cesarean section?
మీరు ఆపరేషన్ ద్వారా ("---------కు") జన్మనిచ్చారా?

☐ Yes   ☐ No

[35] Was your or (NAME)'s health or life at risk at any time during your pregnancy?
మీరు లేక --------- (పేరు), ప్రసవించే సమయంలో ప్రాణాపాయ స్థితి ఎదుర్కొన్నారా?

☐ Yes   ☐ No

[36] What is (NAME)'s gender? --------- (పేరు) లింగం ఏది?

☐ Male   ☐ Female

Thank you very much for your time and help!

Spandana Maternity Care Market Research Study
- Questionnaire II for women who are pregnant for the first time -

[9] In which month of pregnancy are you? మీ గర్భం వచ్చి ఎన్నోనెల?

_____ month [1 to 9]

Interviewer: I would first like to ask you some questions about your person.
మొదటగా వ్యక్తిగత విషయాలు, మీ గురించి కొన్ని ప్రశ్నలు అడగకోరుచున్నాము.

[10] What is your age? మీ వయస్సు ఎంత?

_____ years

[11] What is the highest educational institution you have attended successfully?
మీరు ఉత్తీర్ణులయిన ఉన్నత విద్య ఏది?

☐ Illiterate ☐ Can read but no schooling ☐ 3. Standard ☐ 4.-6. Standard ☐ 7.-10. Standard ☐ College, no graduate ☐ Graduate

[12] What is the highest educational institution your baby's father has attended successfully?
మీ బిడ్డ తండ్రి ఏ ఉన్నత విద్య లో ఉత్తీర్ణులయ్యారు?

☐ Illiterate ☐ Can read but no schooling ☐ 3. Standard ☐ 4.-6. Standard ☐ 7.-10. Standard ☐ College, no graduate ☐ Graduate

[13] Are you member of a Self-Help Group (SHG) in a micro-finance program, chit fund, ROSCA or any similar group lending and saving schemes?
మీరు మైక్రోఫైనాన్స్ ప్రోగ్రామ్ లో సెల్ఫ్‌గ్రూప్ (స్వీయ సహాయ సంస్థ) నందు, చిట్ ఫండ్, ROSCA (రొస్కా) సభ్యత్వం కలదా? ఏదైనా చిన్న మొత్తాల పొదుపు మరియు అప్పుల సంస్థల యందు సభ్యత్వం కలదా?

☐ Yes ☐ No

[14] What is your religion? మీ మతము ఏది?

☐ Hindu ☐ Muslim ☐ Christian ☐ Sikh ☐ Other ☐ None

[15] Do you belong to a scheduled caste, a scheduled tribe, other backward class, or none of these?
మీరు షెడ్యూల్ కాస్ట్/ ట్రైబ్ లేక ఇతర వెనుకబడిన తరగతికి చెందుతారా?

☐ Scheduled caste ☐ Scheduled tribe ☐ Other Backward Class ☐ None of these

[16] Does your community value giving birth at home?
మీ కులంలో ఇంటిలో ప్రసవించే ప్రాముఖ్యత ఉందా?
- [ ] Yes
- [ ] No

[17] Did the majority of your _____ deliver in health facilities?
మీ కుటుంబం సభ్యులలో అధిక సంఖ్యలో ఆరోగ్యకేంద్రాలలో ప్రసవించారా?

family members / relatives	[ ] Yes	[ ] No
friends	[ ] Yes	[ ] No
Self-Help Group/Chit/ROSCA members	[ ] Not Applicable [ ] Yes	[ ] No

Interviewer: Now I would like to ask you some questions about your economic situation.
ఇప్పుడు మీ యొక్క ఆర్థిక స్థోమత స్థితిగతులు అడగతోరుచున్నాము?

[18] What is your household income in Rs per month?
మీ కుటుంబ ఆర్థిక రాబడి మొత్తం నెలకి ఎంత?
- [ ] <1500 Rs.
- [ ] 1500-3000
- [ ] 3001-5000
- [ ] 5001-8000
- [ ] >8000

[19] What is the number of people living in your household?
మీ కుటుంబ సభ్యులు మొత్తం ఎంత మంది?
_____ people

[20] Do you / does your household own land or housing?
మీకు సొంత ఇల్లు లేక భూములు ఉన్నాయా?
- [ ] Yes
- [ ] No

[21] If you / your household owns housing: What is your roof made of?
మీ ఇంటి కప్ప దేనితో నిర్మించబడినది?
- [ ] Thatch
- [ ] Tiles
- [ ] Sheets
- [ ] Slab
- [ ] Not Applicable

[22] Does your household have the following items?
ఈ క్రింది వాటిలో మీ ఇంట్లో ఉన్న వస్తువులు ఏమిటి ?
- [ ] Pressure cookers
- [ ] FAN
- [ ] Television
- [ ] Scooter/ motorcycle
- [ ] Almirah/ Dressing table

[23] In your household, who is the main decision-maker in health related issues?
మీ కుటుంబంలో ఆరోగ్య విషయంలో ఎవరు ముఖ్య సలహాదారులు?

☐ Me   ☐ Husband   ☐ Me & husband jointly   ☐ Others in household   ☐ Others in family   ☐ Others

Interviewer: The following are questions about your pregnancy
ఈ క్రింది ప్రశ్నలు మీ యొక్క గర్భదారణ గురించినవి

[24] Did you receive antenatal care (check-up) for your current pregnancy?
మీరు ప్రస్తుతం గర్భం ధరించుననప్పుడు చికిత్స లభించిందా ?

☐ Yes   ☐ No

[25] <u>If you received antenatal care at least once:</u> How many times did you receive antenatal care during this pregnancy? మీరు ప్రస్తుత గర్భ సమయంలో ఎన్నిసార్లు చికిత్స లభించింది?

Number of times : _____   ☐ Not Applicable

[26] <u>If you received antenatal care at least once:</u> How many months pregnant were you when you first received antenatal care for this pregnancy? మీరు మొదటిసారి గర్భచికిత్స చేసినప్పుడు ఎన్ని నెలలు?

Number of Months: _____   ☐ Not Applicable

[27] How do you plan to finance your delivery? ప్రసవం చేయుటానికి తగిన ఆదాయం ఏది ?

☐ Savings   ☐ Loan from family/ friends   ☐ Supported by in-laws   ☐ SHG loan/ Chit/ ROSCA   ☐ Other: _____ (specify)

[28] What is the travel-distance from your home to the closest health facility of the respective sectors that provides maternity services?
మీ ఇంటినుంచి సమీపంగా ఉన్న ప్రసూతిసేవలు కల్గిఉన్న ఆరోగ్యసంస్థల యొక్క ప్రయాణ దూరం ఎంత?

Govt. hospital distance: _____ km   Pvt. hospital distance: _____ km

[29] What is your expectation of the total costs of your delivery (antenatal care fees, scans, medicines, transport and delivery costs)? మీరు ప్రసవ సమయం వరకు వెచ్చించిన మొత్తం ఎంత?

_____ Rs.

Interviewer: Finally, I would like to ask you four questions about potential complications during pregnancies.
చివరిగా మీబిడ్డ గురించి మరియు గర్భం దరించినప్పుడు ఏమైనా ఎదుర్కొన్న సమస్యలు గురించి అడగకోరుచున్నాము?

[30] Do you have relatives or friends that had a stillbirth or complications during their pregnancy?
మీ యొక్క బంధువులలో లేక స్నేహితులలో గర్భం నశించిపోవుట లేక గర్భదారణ సమయంలో సమస్యలు ఎదుర్కొన్నారా?

☐ Yes ☐ No

[31] Where are you planning to give birth? మీరు ఏ స్థలంలో ప్రసవించాలనుకుంటున్నారు?

☐ at home ☐ Govt. hosp. ☐ Pvt. hospital ☐ Other: _____
(specify)

[34] Are you planning to deliver by cesarean section?
మీరు ఆపరేషన్ ద్వారా జన్మనిస్తారా?

☐ Yes ☐ No

[35] Was your or your baby's health or life at risk at any time during your current pregnancy?
మీరు లేక బిడ్డ ప్రస్తుత గర్భసమయంలో ప్రాణాపాయ స్థితి ఎదుర్కొన్నారా?

☐ Yes ☐ No

[36] Are you aware of the gender of your current pregnancy?
మీకు ప్రస్తుత గర్భలింగం తెలుసా?

☐ Male ☐ Female ☐ Don't know

Thank you very much for your time and help!

UNIVERSITY MEETS MICROFINANCE

edited by PlaNet Finance Deutschland e.V.

ISSN 2190-2291

1. *Pim Engels*
   Mission Drift in Microfinance
   The Influence of Institutional and Country Risk Indicators on the Trade-Off between the Financial and Social Performance of Microfinance Institutions
   ISBN 978-3-8382-0123-8

2. *Thilo Klein*
   Microfinance 2.0
   Group Formation and Repayment Performance in Online Lending Platforms During the US Credit Crunch
   ISBN 978-3-8382-0118-4

3. *Saikumar C. Bharamappanavara*
   The Performance Of Microcredit Organisations
   A Comparative Perspective
   ISBN 978-3-8382-0121-4

4. *Oliver Rogall*
   Microfinance and Vulnerability to Poverty
   The Evidence from Rural Households in Cambodia
   ISBN 978-3-8382-0237-2

5. *Maria Cristina De Lorenzo*
   Microfinance Investment Funds: An analysis of profitability
   ISBN 978-3-8382-0251-8

6. *Sascha Huijsman*
   The Impact of the Current Economic and Financial Crisis on Microfinance
   ISBN 978-3-8382-0235-8

7. *Funmilayo A. Akinosi, Daniel Nordlund, Alejandro Turbay*
   Sustainable Microfinance
   Redefining the Socio-Economic Mission in Microfinance
   ISBN 978-3-8382-0334-8

8. *Anna Custers*
   Furthering Financial Literacy
   Experimental Evidence from a Financial Literacy Training Programme for Microfinance Clients in Bhopal, India
   ISBN 978-3-8382-0337-9

9. *Thilo Klein*
   Why Do India's Urban Poor Choose to Go Private?
   Health Policy Simulations in Slums of Hyderabad
   ISBN 978-3-8382-0238-9

Abonnement

Hiermit abonniere ich die Reihe **University Meets Microfinance (ISSN 2190-2291)**, herausgegeben von PlaNet Finance Deutschland e.V.,

❏ ab Band # 1
❏ ab Band # ___
  ❏ Außerdem bestelle ich folgende der bereits erschienenen Bände:
  #___, ___, ___, ___, ___, ___, ___, ___, ___, ___, ___

❏ ab der nächsten Neuerscheinung
  ❏ Außerdem bestelle ich folgende der bereits erschienenen Bände:
  #___, ___, ___, ___, ___, ___, ___, ___, ___, ___, ___

❏ 1 Ausgabe pro Band   ODER   ❏ ___ Ausgaben pro Band

Bitte senden Sie meine Bücher zur versandkostenfreien Lieferung innerhalb Deutschlands an folgende Anschrift:

Vorname, Name: _____

Straße, Hausnr.: _____

PLZ, Ort: _____

Tel. (für Rückfragen): _____ *Datum, Unterschrift:* _____

Zahlungsart

❏ *ich möchte per Rechnung zahlen*
❏ *ich möchte per Lastschrift zahlen*

bei Zahlung per Lastschrift bitte ausfüllen:

Kontoinhaber: _____

Kreditinstitut: _____

Kontonummer: _____ Bankleitzahl: _____

Hiermit ermächtige ich jederzeit widerruflich den *ibidem*-Verlag, die fälligen Zahlungen für mein Abonnement der Reihe **University Meets Microfinance** von meinem oben genannten Konto per Lastschrift abzubuchen.

Datum, Unterschrift: _____

Abonnementformular entweder **per Fax** senden an: **0511 / 262 2201** oder 0711 / 800 1889
oder als **Brief** an: *ibidem*-Verlag, Leuschnerstr. 40, 30457 Hannover oder
als e-mail an: ibidem@ibidem-verlag.de

ibidem-Verlag

Melchiorstr. 15

D-70439 Stuttgart

info@ibidem-verlag.de

www.ibidem-verlag.de
www.ibidem.eu
www.edition-noema.de
www.autorenbetreuung.de

Zeitfracht Medien GmbH
Ferdinand-Jühlke-Straße 7,
99095 - DE, Erfurt
produktsicherheit@zeitfracht.de